# I Surrender All

# I Surrender All

A 5 Step Recovery Program

## JOHN FURR

authorHOUSE®

*AuthorHouse™*
*1663 Liberty Drive*
*Bloomington, IN 47403*
*www.authorhouse.com*
*Phone: 1-800-839-8640*

*First published by AuthorHouse     08/12/2011*

*ISBN: 978-1-4634-8734-8 (sc)*
*ISBN: 978-1-4634-8733-1 (dj)*
*ISBN: 978-1-4634-8732-4 (ebk)*

*Library of Congress Control Number: 2011914558*

*Printed in the United States of America*

# Preface

My name is John Furr, but I have always gone by Jay. This book is based on my life story, which unfolded as I battled addiction. What you're about to read is truthful and very direct. I have through inspiration created a five-step recovery program. It is a faith-based program that requires you to put your trust in God and know that you can be healed. It will take you on a journey as you battle your addiction. Unlike the traditional twelve-step programs you're used to, in this program you will be healed from your addiction. You will not ever refer to yourself as an addict; rather, you will be a new creation in the sight of God. The five steps are as follows:

1. Identify your god.
2. Pray without ceasing.
3. Give it all to God.
4. Don't take it back.
5. Expect the miracle.

These steps constitute a nontraditional approach to treating addiction. They outline my life story, which is a rags-to-riches, jailed-to-free adventure that will take your breath away. It takes you inside prison walls and through the daily struggle involved when trying to beat addiction. I am not a drug counselor, but I am extremely qualified to have written this book, so I hope you enjoy the story.

For over fifteen years, I have battled my addiction to meth and cocaine. It has not been an easy battle, but I have survived. I have attempted to summarize my path to sobriety in the five basic steps, which have helped me stay clean. If you will follow them and do everything discussed in the book, you will succeed. I have been right where you are—jobless, homeless, doing whatever it took to get my dope. I would do anything. I gave up my kids to do my dope. It didn't matter to me. I was unable to feel for others, but now I am where you can be.

This book is a unique approach to sobriety; in fact, it takes the most nontraditional approach I have ever seen. It basically helps you see that you're not an addict anymore. Rather, your disease (addiction) can be cured and placed into 100 percent remission through those five simple steps. It requires a mind open to what you read, a belief in God and in Jesus, and the belief that God will heal you. If you trust in what I am saying, then when you finish this book, you will have the knowledge you need to stop using and never pick up a drug again. This I promise.

I hope you will take from this book what is needed to begin a life worth living and hold on to these simple steps to ensure that you never use drugs again. All the steps mentioned have worked in my personal experience. I am not a drug counselor, nor am I a medical worker or a prophet of God. I am simply the voice God chose to speak these simple steps to try to help others through this book, written with his inspiration. This book takes an approach to drug abuse that will actually *heal* you.

I have seen lives destroyed, and I almost destroyed my own. But I never saw the happiness that awaited me until I began to live a life of meaning and, in return, to build the relationships once thought impossible. I practice these steps daily, and I have had my entire life restored tenfold. I have been to hell and back but have been spared by God to share with you the story of that road you don't want to go down. I have lost my freedom on three separate occasions and damn near lost my life on two. It is so important for you to open your heart to what you are reading. Listen to that still, small voice as it prompts you regarding what to do. By ignoring it, you will take much longer to finally get it.

Many addiction-recovery programs out there will tell you how to accomplish certain things in your effort to beat drugs and alcohol, but that is not what I am trying to get across to you. My goal in writing this book is for you to gain an intimate relationship with God that goes beyond stopping the use of drugs. What I want for you is an understanding that God is so real, so powerful, so loving, and so involved in every step you take that this will be life changing. By learning and recognizing God's presence, you will take from this book all the necessary tools to literally be able to talk to your father and know that he is listening.

# Chapter 1

## The Promise That Awaits

March 23, 2009, was what I would say was one of the most powerful nights in my life. I was getting used to my freedom; I had just been released from a county jail in Utah and was in what's called the reentry program—basically a halfway house. I was awaiting sentencing for a gun charge that I thought had been dismissed, but I found out that it had been refiled as a felony. I had not been charged with anything since all my drug charges in 1999. I hadn't been in jail since 2002, and I was in a place unlike any other I had experienced in my life. I was actually sober for the first time since my 2007 relapse in Hawaii. I was unemployed, broke, and totally dependent on my faith in God for the first time on the outside. I had depended on God in jail, but it had been a long time. I am telling you this because it was on this night that I finally realized that God was actively involved in my day-to-day life, right down to the decisions I was making about my life. It was at this time that God promised me that if I would follow his teachings, I would prosper. I was facing more time in prison, a possibility that was, to say the least, unattractive to me. I had thought that my life of crime was over, but when I relapsed, it started all over again. I was trying so hard to not relapse into my drug addiction, and I really wanted to figure out where God wanted me—or, for that matter, *if* he wanted me anymore. I was lost but thought I could somehow pull something off in court that would save me one more time. I mean, I really wanted to change. The time I spent behind bars apparently hadn't worked, so I wanted this time to be a fresh start.

I decided to ask the judge for assignment to a rehab program in California called Teen Challenge. It's a yearlong program but can be longer if needed. Participants can go to the program's Bible college for another year, graduate, and become staff members at any one of their more than two hundred centers. I really was excited about this possibility.

I was attending church regularly—weekly, in fact—reading my Bible daily, and doing everything I thought was necessary. I would walk through town every day in an attempt to find employment, but God wasn't speaking to me at all. My then mentor, or second mom—who is now my mother-in-law—was doing all she knew to do to point out where I was messing up in my thinking. She kept saying something to me that didn't make any sense at all. I'll never forget how she would say over and over again, "Son, *surrender!*"

I had owned a transmission repair center and had expanded it to seven locations. At one point in my life, I had more money than I knew what to do with, and yet there I sat in a hole-in-the-wall, one-room, government-assisted halfway house with no job, no hope, no car, no money, and no prospects. And she was telling me that I needed to surrender. She would come by daily to check on me, and most of the time she would even invite me to her home to eat or would somehow bring leftovers almost nightly. I can't begin to convey how important her visits were. I had not yet gotten my food stamps, and food was nice. By taking that worry off of me, she offered me a huge relief that's almost unexplainable. She would also pick me up and take me to do my laundry. I remember one time when she picked me up and took me to a thrift store called Deseret Industries, which is the Mormon church's version of Goodwill or the Salvation Army. She spent almost the entire day getting me free clothes and bedding. I had only one change of clothes when I was released because I had been arrested in Seattle and then taken to Utah, where my charges had been filed. What a bold and God-loving person she was. I believed that she didn't have a clue about what I was going through, that she couldn't know how much God had been humbling me over the previous several months. Boy, was I wrong. God had chosen her to be the person to help place and keep me on the right track.

When you have nowhere else to turn and you least expect it, God will appear there. He can appear in the smile of a child or as a passerby on the street. My mentor took me under her wing and showed me what love is supposed to be like in a family. She was of humble means, but she never missed a chance to feed me a meal, nor did she ever neglect to pick me up for Bible study or any church activity. She truly led by her example of what a walk with Christ looks like. But all she kept saying to me was, "Son, surrender."

I was not totally clear on what she meant by that until one night when she came by and played a song called "Surrender" by Janis Freeman. This song was written during the recovery of an addict who was from the same area in Utah. I remember as plain as day the feelings I had when she played this song. Tears began to run down my face, and then I began sobbing uncontrollably. I was weeping. I couldn't believe that those words were being sung by an angel who, like myself, had once fallen from grace and now was being used by God himself, telling me to surrender all to God.

The song "Surrender" is copyrighted and available for you to download for free—courtesy of the artist, Janis Freeman—on our website, http://heavenlyoaksretreat.com. I placed the song there for readers to hear so that it could help set the tone for the rest of the book. This entire book could be about certain people and the roles they have played in my life, but it is not about me and my life; it's about you and your life. It's about how God awaits your call. It's about how, if you simply ask, it will simply be given to you. I had never been able to understand that concept until recently: God's desire is for your dreams of happiness and success to be fulfilled.

It's like when you see your son hit his first home run or watch your daughter graduate with honors from college or make the winning shot in overtime. It's a feeling unlike anything other. When you feel so good about something, it warms you up inside. That's the feeling I want you to try to feel when you read that we were created to bring joy unto God. He delights in our seeking him, and he finds pleasure in our success. So if we were created to bring him joy, how do we go about doing that? It's simply in the way we choose to seek him in anything that we do, and that's done by including him in everything we do.

It's my goal that after you read this book, you will be better than when you began and will have healed from the most dangerous disease on this earth, addiction. But most important, it's my prayer that you begin the most intimate relationship available to mankind, that involving the love of the heavenly father. It is my prayer that you will begin this relationship that is so long overdue. Words can't express and tears can't measure the love that is awaiting you from the god of all things created.

Look around you—everything you see has been created by him simply for your enjoyment. Pets were made for your comfort, and mountains, lakes, streams, oceans—all of these things were made by him for you. If that doesn't blow your mind, then nothing will. So please begin this book with the following prayer, which I feel will help you set the tone. I do encourage you to set the book down from time to time and plead with God, praying for his presence to be with you.

> God, I thank you for the chance you have given me and my family to be a part of this book, *I Surrender All*. It truly has shown me that you will enter people's lives as far as they will let you in, right down to even whispering to them in that still, small voice what to say and when to say it. Father, in reading this book and praying this prayer, I have made the first step necessary to getting better. God, I ask you to please allow me to feel your presence now. Let me know what I have come to learn, which is that you are real and that you're an amazing god who is so anxiously awaiting my cry for your help. God, show me how simple life is supposed to be. Show me how to identify you, and most of all, God, please send down angels to take from me all of my worries. Please, by your power, fulfill the promise that if I will take on the blood of your son, Jesus Christ, I will be healed. I ask that it be recorded in heaven and that this promise will come true for me. I do not doubt you, Lord God, nor do I worry about the promise's truthfulness. I call upon you as Moses called upon you to deliver his people from bondage. God, please deliver me from bondage—the bondage of drugs and earthly things this life has to offer. I know I am not Moses, but I am your

child, and you love me just as much as you loved Moses.
Please deliver me. In the name of Jesus I pray, amen.


After a brief stint in the army, I found myself with an addiction to pills. It started out with a simple knee surgery that went bad when I was in my mid to late twenties, and it turned into a full-blown addiction in less than a year. I would take ten to twenty pills a day—Lortab, Lorcet 10/650, Xanax, and Soma—and tell myself it was okay because they were legal. These were medicines prescribed by my doctor. I had had two knee surgeries, and all I had to do was show the scar to get a prescription. It just so happens that I was in the wrong doctor's office at the right time. Then they weren't enough. In fact, they became gateway drugs to my drugs of choice—meth and cocaine.

It's so important that you understand that I wasn't looking for an addiction at all. I had two beautiful children and was a full-time student along with my then wife. We were trying to live the American dream, get educated, and begin our lives together. Our wedding was held in a Mormon temple, and I was trying to live what I thought was a Christian life. But I was truly suffering from this knee injury. It seemed that all my days consisted of was physical therapy and classes.

Once I started taking the pills, I really liked them. They took my mind off of the more serious issues, like bills and studies, but just like that, what I was taking wasn't enough. I wanted to get higher. I was a full-blown addict. I have been in several programs, from faith-based to in-your-face-based, and have found very little success. I actually had no problem getting sober. The problem was living the life that followed. That's what I really struggled with. Nothing worked for me. In one program, I was classified as having a polysubstance dependency, which means that I was unable to function without some kind of drug in my system.

## Accepting the Unacceptable

I was raised in the South, and believe it or not, most of the raising was right. My mother came from a very large and close family that is unlike any other I have ever been around. The brothers and sisters loved each other amazingly and, as a result, loved their nephews and nieces as if they were their own children. So when I tell you they were close, I mean that I had uncles who were like fathers to me and aunts who were like mothers. I had my favorite ones, but altogether they were amazing, each and every one of them. In fact, I learned the value of work not from my father but from my uncle Joe. He taught me that honesty and hard work would get me anywhere I wanted to go in life. We worked together every summer, and when I was only twenty-one, we were partners in an asphalt-paving company until his death only one year after we had opened our doors.

So, unlike a lot of addicts, I didn't have a distant family, especially not on my mom's side. My father's family, though, was larger and didn't come close to comparing to my mom's family. I still to this day have aunts and uncles on my father's side that I have never met. In the pages to follow, you will get to know a lot about my life and the way I was raised. You will read things I have never shared with anyone. Knowing that my mother's family consisted of what you would call gypsies or travelers—you know, the guys who knock on your door asking about paving your driveway with leftover asphalt—will help you understand that because I was the one who used the drugs, I had to accept the consequences no matter what. I had always felt different, but nothing prepared me for the realization of how different I truly was. I wasn't raised to use drugs. Never in my entire childhood did any of my friends offer me drugs or use drugs, to my knowledge. None of us seemed destined to be addicts when we grew up.

All of my childhood friends were as normal as could be. I don't know if any of them have experienced the pain of addiction that I have or the sorrow and regret that comes along with it. I was baptized as a Latter-day Saint, also known as a Mormon. My mother converted to Mormonism before I was even born. I attended all the church meetings, starting with the primary level, then the priesthood, then a two-year mission, and finally marriage in the temple—twice. For those of you who are not Mormons, being married in the temple is the most coveted practice of the church because doing so, Mormons believe, seals the spouses as a family for all time and eternity. Marrying in the temple is an honor for practicing Mormons. At the time, I knew who God was but had never had that personal relationship that I needed. I am not slamming the way I was raised; I am merely pointing out that I had never had Christ in my corner of life.

Later in the book, I mention that I blame my addiction on my lack of a relationship with God. There is proof of this in my experience: every time I relapsed or got high was a time that I didn't have Christ in my life. It came about so suddenly, that falling away from the light. First, you stop kneeling when you pray, and then you stop praying altogether. In the way I was raised, people were taught to respect God by kneeling. Therefore, I have always chosen to kneel when I pray because I want God to know that I am in complete submission to him, that I love him so much that I bow at his feet. But when you eventually stop praying altogether, you find yourself being in the wrong mix of things. Let me try to explain. If you're used to doing things a certain way, like I was—which was taking everything to God in prayer and living a life with God in it—and all of a sudden you lose that lifestyle, things seem to lose their value to you, and before you know it, you're lying to people, testing the waters that you shouldn't even be near. I hope the five steps in this book will inspire you to gain and to maintain that personal relationship with your savior.

## My Approach to Identifying Your God

The first step, identifying your god, is so important. I want to share a story with you. I moved to Honolulu, Hawaii, to run two transmission centers for the largest transmission company in the world. I had just made a score of a drug called ice—it was the best score I had made on the island—and was entering day seventeen of a bender. A bender is a stretch of consecutive days that a user is "up" while using methamphetamines. It's like bending a piece of metal until it reaches its breaking point. In other words, I was beginning day seventeen of no sleep. Having battled drugs for the previous ten years, I had gone off the deep end yet again. I was forty years old and going through another crisis in my life. I was on marriage number five, this one to a twenty-year-old prostitute, and job number four for that year. I was making upwards of one hundred thousand dollars a year but didn't have enough money to buy food.

This particular morning, as I prepared my morning blast (a method of shooting up), I was surprised to wake up in the back of an ambulance. Frantically searching for a familiar face, I was dismayed that I could not find my wife anywhere. I found out later that she was in the parking lot trying to score more drugs. Anyway, I remember coming to in the back of the ambulance and seeing the fear in the EMT's eyes as she speedily worked on me. Her fear made me even more afraid.

As I looked up into the technician's eyes, I started to ask her what was going on only to realize that I couldn't speak. My fear was unimaginable. I couldn't even see her well, only through my left eye. As the words slurred out of my mouth, the EMT told me, "Relax. We think you're having a stroke." When we reached the hospital, I was wheeled in and seen by the doctor. It was his conclusion that I had experienced what he classified as a mini stroke, and he proceeded to admit me. But before he did, he asked the nurse to leave and pulled the curtain closed. He said that I would most likely regain the vision in my right eye and that my speech was already getting better. He said, "During some of the tests, you tested positive for meth and cocaine, and I also noticed the severe track marks on your arms." I was surprised he had noticed them. I would put on makeup, wear long sleeves—hell, I even got tattoos to cover them—but he still was able to see them. I often look back on when I first started using drugs. I thought that the guys who shot up were true junkies. Four weeks after I began using, I became a true junkie.

The doctor was unlike anyone I had ever met in my life. For some reason, he really seemed to care. As he sat down on my bed, he began to explain that every time I used drugs the way I did, intravenously, it was like peeing on an electric fence. I might be getting high, but my heart was taking the brunt of it. My heart was literally being shot up, not just my mind. It would only take me a year and six months to truly understand what he was trying to get through my thick skull. He got up off the bed, looked me in the eye, and said, "Son, I'll let you stay for detox. I want you to know that I understand the mess you're in, so if you want me to help you, I'll help you." I lay in the bed waiting to be admitted, and it's sad, but when you're high, you don't think too clearly.

As he left, I started thinking more about his offer, but I couldn't help but think that he might call the cops. I was so scared that I jerked the IV out and left the hospital. I then had my wife call my drug dealer and tell him to pick us up. We were thirty-five minutes from our apartment in Waikiki. We lived above the shop where I worked, so I couldn't go there. We went to the dope house instead. That entire night, I continually watched everyone around me as they got high. It was something I will never forget. It almost felt like time had slowed to a standstill. I looked at one of my friends and realized how rough he looked, and I got up, went to the mirror, and looked into it. That's when I realized how rough I looked—unshaven, thin. It looked like my eyes were in the back of my head. I stared, and as I looked, I saw nothing. I saw absolutely nothing. It was like my soul was gone, like I couldn't feel happy or sad. I had looked rough before, but never in my life had I looked in the mirror and seen nothing. I stood there, soulless, and for the first time in my life, I knew what it meant to reach rock bottom.

I also want you to know that my "qualifications" are as follows: there is not one thing shy of murder that I haven't been through, tried, or done. But none of that is a part of my life now, and it doesn't have to be a part of yours. The purpose of this book is to help you feel God and take these five steps so you can actually become what you were made to be. In step one, you may consider reading the Bible to help you identify your god. When people go to Alcoholics Anonymous, they are required to pick up AA's "big book," in which they read stories intended to help them begin working through their twelve steps. Well, I am telling you to pick up the biggest book and begin to read stories that tell what God is like, what he has done in the past, and what he continues to do now in our lives. I also feel that praying, which leads into step two, is a requirement in identifying your god. I have found strength in attending a local church, where I see how other people lead "normal" lives and become encouraged to strive for what they have.

Now, back to my Hawaii story. I don't know if you have been to Hawaii, but it's one of the most beautiful and amazing places known to man. God was truly having a good day when it was made. It has a great culture, people with outstanding values, and some of the most beautiful scenery your eyes will ever see. Hawaii, unlike any other place in the world, will literally take your breath away on a daily basis. The sunsets actually are what you see in the movies. As I look back, I am still amazed at how heavenly Hawaii truly is.

With all of this around me, I still chose to get high. On the same night that I fled the ER, I walked around trying to clear my head and ended up walking on the beach—the world-famous Waikiki Beach. And—can you believe it?—God didn't appear to me. I mean, there I was, broken-hearted and at my rock bottom, and no vision came to me. It's strange. Instead, God chose to speak to me in the smallest, simplest ways.

With the waves going in and out, I watched families on the beach as they threw the Frisbee, strangers smiling as they walked by, children playing, tourists filling up the resorts, and people with new clothes, and I heard the sounds of laughter. All of this made me realize just how alone I really was. I finally saw how I had allowed my addiction to alienate me from everything. I had lost all five of my children to my addiction. I was five thousand miles away from anybody I really knew, and the Lord told me to run—run as fast as I could.

It was then that I began my prayer: "God, make me physically sick at the very sight of drugs." I prayed this prayer for weeks, for months, before it finally became true. In the Bible, the Lord tells Jacob, "I have made you, you are my servant;

Israel, I will not forget you" (Is. 44:21 NIV). If the Bible says God made me and knows me, then it must be true. But I needed to be pushed. I had a great job, and—as I have mentioned—it was Hawaii. How could I leave?

I got back to my apartment to find all my clothes in the street. I rented my apartment from my employer, and he had kicked me to the curb after finding out that I had relapsed. I picked my stuff up, made a phone call, and lined up a job in Seattle with my old boss. In my line of work, if you're a good salesman, then you're always in demand, no matter what drama you may bring with you.

After hitchhiking to the airport while dragging three bags, I got to the Hawaiian Airlines counter ready to board the plane, and the clerk said, "That will be eighty-seven dollars." I became frantic. "Eighty-seven dollars for what?" I asked, and the clerk replied, "For your baggage, sir." Little did I know that this was a new policy. I held my head, not knowing what to do, not having a single penny left to my name. I made the decision to leave my bags behind just as the person at the counter said, "Sir, here is your boarding pass. Your baggage has been taken care of."

An elderly gentleman approached me and said, "Nothing in this life is too big that prayer can't make it small." He said he had felt compelled to take care of my luggage and wished me luck. I headed to Seattle and an unknown future.

# Chapter 2

## Step 1: Identify Your God

As addicts, we struggle with identifying our god more than any other thing in the world. Your god can be money, possessions, and/ or beautiful things. That night in 2007, on the plane headed back to the mainland, my god had yet to show his face. Let me make one thing clear: identifying your god is not an easy task. I remember sitting on that flight thinking, *Am I really done this time? I'm going back to Seattle where I relapsed the first time, to the same friends, the same job, making more money. What do I do?* I then found myself praying that same prayer: "God, please make me physically sick of the sight of drugs."

With a marriage that was at a dead end and biting my nails every day to stay sober, I needed help. I remember going to the restroom at my job in north Seattle and kneeling on my knees, saying, "God, please don't let this be another two or three week sober thing." At the center where I was working, I could see the only entrance to the parking lot right when I walked out of the restroom. Imagine my surprise when I looked out the window to see more than a dozen federal and local police officers with guns drawn, looking for me. When they found me, I protested, "There is no way this could be for me." They stated that they were there to arrest me on charges stemming from a prior arrest, made some two years before, that had been refiled as a felony. I had a no-bail situation, meaning that I would be staying in jail regardless of how much money or how many friends I had, and would be extradited to Utah. *Extradition* basically means that you're stuck waiting on someone to send for you, which could take months.

I didn't know it then, but my god was about to identify himself in my life. I had reached the end. I had nothing left inside me—nothing at all. I mean, there was no hope, no way I was going to continue to live the life I had been living. I had finally reached the point of being sick and tired of being sick and tired. I needed to end a marriage, I needed to end my job, and I needed a drastic change.

I had lost my freedom once before. In fact, that is when I found God for the first time in my life. They call it a jailhouse conversion—you proclaim Jesus, get out, and forget Jesus. Well, I hadn't forgotten him totally; I had only misplaced him. I can't exactly explain it, but I felt safe again. (I want to make every attempt to avoid making this book be about my criminal career as an addict, but for you to understand where I am coming from, a little background is necessary. I mention more in the chapters to come about my past jail time.) I finally knew that I was not going to be getting high anytime soon. Am I actually saying God put me back in jail? Is that even possible? I answer that question with another: is this the same God who put Daniel in the lions' den and allowed Joseph to be sold into slavery? Did he not do this all throughout Bible times? Yes, I am saying that God identified himself to me and put me in jail, this time in Seattle.

You see, there are times in life when you will become overwhelmed or depressed and even feel that life has treated you unfairly. When these times come, it's easier to fall victim to self-pity and get that "poor me" attitude than to stay positive. When such times have come in my life, they were almost a guarantee that I would get high. It is times like these, however, that God is anxiously waiting to reveal himself to us so that we can gain the serenity needed to succeed. I can recall many times in my life when I felt mistreated, but only in the most recent years have I been able to take the knowledge of who my god is—the same god who created this earth and is found in the Bible—and realize that every single thing in my life, down to the very air I breathe, is accounted for. Doesn't that blow your mind to know that every single breath we take has been accounted for by our god? From experience, I know this to be true.

So, in summary, step one—identifying your god—can be done simply by looking for him in the right places. The first place to look for him is on your knees. Identify him by the actions that you take. I mean truly look for him in the things you're doing in your life, like helping people, attending church, not cussing, not lying, not leading a criminal lifestyle whatsoever. I can promise you that God is not a mystical wind blowing in the air. He is not a higher power; he is an actual living god. He is your father. He created you, so he is your actual father.

In other programs, people will tell you that he can be anything just as long as he is your higher power. I'm telling you that in this five-step program, he is God, the eternal father in heaven. He is the father of heaven and earth who created man in his own image. That is the god I am talking about and want you to see. He is also a god of compassion, faithfulness, kindness, happiness, and love. When you identify your god, it will be as clear as the nose on your face. You will have no doubts. The god I am speaking of to you will place certain things and certain people in your life and in your path that will do anything to see that you succeed.

# Chapter 3

## Step 2: Pray Without Ceasing

Now that you have identified your god, I cannot sufficiently stress to you how important it is to keep him identified because this next step, pray without ceasing, is the first move toward serving your god through prayer. In the Bible, the Book of Isaiah says,

> I have called you back from the ends of the earth saying, you are my servant for I have chosen you and will not throw you away. Don't be afraid, I am with you. Don't be discouraged, for I am your god. I will strengthen you and help you, I will hold you up with my victorious right hand. (41:9-10 New Living Translation)

Throughout the Bible, God promises us that if we will merely ask, it will be given. God has also promised us that he will crush our enemies. What greater enemy is there in your life right now than addiction? We can't destroy it by ourselves, but we can with God's help. He will hold your hand and help you all the way. God will redeem us and make us whole again. He will take the dreams of using away, and we will lose interest in the people who are bad for us as we begin leading godly lives.

When I was going through the steps myself, I had prayed before but only when I needed something. I would never pray when I didn't need anything. I had read more books on prayer than most people have read books of any kind, but never had I figured out what the phrase "pray without ceasing" meant.

Finally, I found myself sitting in the King County jail in downtown Seattle. I can remember how in love with the city I had become. In a two-year period, I had moved back and forth between Hawaii and Seattle four times, trying to outrun God and my addiction. It seemed at the time that I was going to beat this addiction. With every move, I would put together two, sometimes three, weeks of clean living, but eventually I would step back into the same path and wind up high. I don't know if you have ever been to jail, but let me tell you, it can be a living hell or it can be one of the godliest experiences of your life. But the bigger the city is, the more inmates there are, and with more inmates comes a scarier and more dangerous environment. I never dreamed that jail would once again define my future.

Let me explain: when a person is processed in, he has to see the doctor, who determines his health status to decide whether he will a) become an inmate worker, b) become a trustee, c) just be in general population, or d) be released to the medical unit. It was at this point that the female intern doctor told me that I had high blood pressure and that she had picked up on a small heart murmur. I had no clue how powerful that little irregular heartbeat would become in my life. You may recall that my prayer was "Father, please make me physically sick at the sight of drugs."

When in jail, the day consists of sitting around and playing cards or doing push-ups. Inmates tend to have a lot of free time on their hands. So that's when I began to pray like never before. I am not talking about a prayer like one a traditional Christian would pray; I am saying that out of the sixteen waking hours per day, I would spend at least fourteen hours talking to my father in heaven. I would ask him to not let me fail this time and to not allow my mind to wander back to the ways of my past life. All I wanted to do was talk to my god, my father in heaven. If one of the guards had seen me, I am sure I would have gotten a trip to medical for a mental health evaluation. This memory is strong in my mind because I can never forget everything that was going on in my life. It was also during this incarceration that my estranged wife and I called it quits and that every friend and my boss washed their hands of me. When I was extradited, I had one change of clothes, no friends, no wife, no money, and finally nothing but God to rely on. It truly was amazing. Once again, it felt like being born all over.

I had prayed nonstop for change in my life and continued this prayer until I was right where God wanted me to be: in his arms and will-less. It was on a Monday afternoon, forty-two days from the day the federal marshals held me at gunpoint, when I began my trip to Utah. It's about twelve to sixteen hours of driving from Seattle to Salt Lake City, but it took us twenty-two days and three hours to get there. We must have stopped at almost every county jail between Seattle and Salt Lake City.

I look back now and realize that every stop was needed. It was as if God had preplanned every one. I would meet or bunk with someone who needed to hear my witness. It was through that experience that God and I grew so close that my life was changed forever. What I mean by close is that I wanted to seek him more than ever, and I felt him wanting me to seek him more than ever. I felt like my insides were glowing, like a new creation was being born.

I would also meet deputies and inmates who needed to hear my testimony, and for the first time I wasn't afraid to share it with them. God had saved me, and I wanted everyone to know it. I was the happiest inmate in the van, without a doubt, even though I was in custody. I prayed nonstop. I would hold the hands of accused murderers and share some of the most powerful testimony of how Christ had spared my life. I would pray with them as they would weep, and they would feel God's presence and accept Jesus as their lord and savior. I would tell everyone that Jesus was real and that I was finally healed from an addiction to drugs, and they would listen. I had prayed this upon myself, and I was okay with it. That's right; I was completely okay with where I was and what I was doing for the first time in my entire existence on this earth. It's a feeling that words cannot begin to explain.

Praying without ceasing can be the most powerful experience because it rewards you with intimacy with God. By praying, you are in constant communication with your father, your counselor, your mentor. I don't know about you, but when I am building a relationship with someone, we talk, and in the course of our talking, we get to know each other and a relationship is born. It is no different with God. You are beginning a relationship by praying to God, by talking to him, by getting to know his will and finding out if he is there or not.

In 1 Thessalonians 5:17-22, God commands us to pray without ceasing:

> Never stop praying, be thankful in all your circumstances for this is God's will for you who belong to Christ Jesus, do not stifle the holy spirit. Do not scoff at prophecies but test everything that is said. Hold on to what is good. Stay away from everything that is evil.

I can remember finally getting to Utah. I had arrived once again; I was back in a Utah county jail. Five years earlier, I had spent a year there, so I knew a lot of the staff; believe it or not, a lot of the same inmates were still there. It seems to me—and I have learned from experience—that the jail system is a revolving door. Once you go in and get out, it is only a matter of time before you go back in. I surveyed inmates at the county jail in my home county, along with a deputy jailer, and found that 92 percent were being held on drug charges or charges stemming from drug or alcohol addiction.

I have a friend named Jim with whom I had been in jail years earlier. I can honestly tell you that he is one of my best friends, but we are no good for each other, or to each other, for that matter. It just seems that every time we get together, one is sober and the other one is not. And the one who isn't gets the other to relapse. Let me give you an example. We spent over a year together in county jail, and he got out first. He had been out for about five months when I was released. The day I was released, his wife picked me up from the bus stop only to tell me that Jim was back in. Over the next four years, we relapsed together more than a half dozen times. When I talk about relapse, I mean *relapse*. I remember walking into a twelve-step program meeting in a little town called Springville, Utah. I had two days of being clean and sober under my belt and was desperately trying to stay clean. But wouldn't you know, there was my friend getting his one-year chip. As soon as the meeting was over, I whispered in his ear, "Let's me and you go for coffee." As you can imagine, he and I went for a six-week "coffee break."

A year and a half after that relapse, I was in another small town called Provo, Utah, getting my own one-year chip when—you guessed it—Jim asked me to join him for coffee. That coffee break lasted more than a year. Make no mistake: it was not Jim's fault that I chose to get high, nor was it my fault that he chose to get high. We were each responsible for ourselves.

The reason I chose to include Jim in this book is to show you that Satan will do everything in his power to keep you from being everything you're supposed to be. He will use friends, family, or whatever is at his disposal to take you down. Another reason for discussing Jim is that—if you remember reading earlier—when I had just arrived in the county jail after my three-week bus ride, he was not only in the same county jail as I was; he was also my cellmate once again. We were in a jail with over seven hundred inmates, and he was in a two-man cell with me. Just like old times, or was it?

I can remember how excited I was to be around him. I hadn't spoken to him in quite a while. It was such a comfort knowing he was there, but what an awful, trying time it was too. Our first and only night together, he talked about our drug days. Eventually, after he had fallen asleep, I got on my knees and quietly prayed to God, "In the name of Jesus, take this temptation away from me." I prayed without ceasing till I fell asleep on my knees.

The next day, at about ten thirty in the morning, his name was called over the intercom, and he was taken out of the cell. About thirty minutes later, the cell door opened, and in he came. Smiling from ear to ear, he said, "Man, can you believe it? They're releasing me on home confinement due to overcrowding." This was January, and his release date wasn't scheduled until July of that year. And yet he was going home. As soon as he rolled up his stuff and we hugged each other's neck, I dropped to my knees and thanked God for answering my prayers. I said, "Wow. You're really listening. This time must be for real." Whenever a person is incarcerated, his cellmate makes a world of difference. My next cellmate wanted to learn more about God. I was in jail that time for a charge that had been filed three years earlier. Why? Because my god wanted me to be in complete and total submission to his will. He had shown his face to me and made my situation such that I could turn myself to no one else but him.

I began doing what I thought I was supposed to do: I began studying his word. On one particular day, I noticed a guy walking by himself along the upper tier, and I decided to see if I could befriend him. Without mentioning any names, let me tell you a little bit about him. First, he was sentenced to five years in a federal prison for committing perjury on a witness stand. Come to find out, it was in reference to the murder of a missing teenager that had occurred some twenty years earlier. This young man had no clue about what was ahead of him. He was scared of his own shadow, or at least that's what I thought. But I soon realized that God had placed him where he was as well. For the next two months, I spent every free minute out of my cell walking, talking, and witnessing about Jesus. If you'll remember, I had been in the same county jail years before, and that is where my relationship with Christ truly began. It's funny that when you are incarcerated, you tend to do a lot of praying. If someone has anything in his life that is good, he must have prayed it upon himself. So when I say to pray without ceasing, I'm literally telling you to never stop, to always keep a prayer in your heart, and to kneel before God at least twice a day, in the morning when you wake and before you go to sleep at night.

# Chapter 4

## Step Three: Give It All to God

Let me begin by defining what *all* means. When you're praying, you have to have faith that someone is listening to what you're saying. You have to believe that if you're saying, "God, help me with my drug problem. I am weak, and I give this over to you for your help," then he will help you. It is hard to have that much faith, but you must. I can't tell you how many times I have given it all over to God only to get up off my knees and take it all back. There is an art to giving everything up to God. In 1 John 1:9 (American Standard Version), the writer tells us, "But if we confess our sins, he is faithful and righteous to forgive us of our sins and to cleanse us of all unrighteousness."

Drug abuse and addiction are not just diseases but also sins. As we take those things into our bodies, we are sinning. I don't know of a single program that will tell you addiction is a sin; they tell you it is strictly a disease. But I am here to tell you that it is both. Your first instinct as an addict is to take an "I can do this" attitude. You think, *I don't need to confess this. I can handle this.* That is where you start to go wrong.

Other step programs ask participants to make a list of the people they have harmed and to, if possible, attempt to make amends. I think that in their politically correct way they are saying the same thing that I am saying—that it is a sin to abuse drugs. The only difference is that I am saying that you have to confess it to God to allow him to cleanse you of your sins. Would it blow your mind if I told you that the debt you have accrued from all you have done wrong is paid in full already? I mean that for every single person you have harmed or hurt, the check has been picked up and paid for you. Jesus Christ gave his life for all of your sins, and the Bible tells us that we are saved by grace. You have enough faith to believe that relationships can be restored, and they will. People will be able to tell what kind of person you are by the way you live your life. This concept doesn't allow you to intentionally harm others and think you're going to be all right. Rather, when you're trying to get sober, focus on you and not on anything else. Let Christ pay for your sins, and start living a life that reflects the knowledge that you're saved by the grace of God. That's the beauty of this program: you don't have to stand up and say, "Hi, my name is Jay, and I'm an addict." Instead, you can simply know that you're healed and that you're a new creation in the eyes of God.

The next few pages could be the most life-changing pages you will ever read. I have spoken of it time and again, and now you need to know that I am where I am because I confessed my sins and accepted Jesus Christ in my life as my personal savior, sponsor, and new drug counselor. This program is nothing new; rather, it has a different twist. It is being written out of the true inspiration of a former addict who is not in recovery but has been healed by the grace and mercy of Jesus.

I don't want to lose you here. Please listen to me. No matter what faith you are or what church you attend, this is one on one between you and God only. The church or faith is the way you choose to worship your god; I am merely trying to tell you that where you're at now, there is hope. Help is not on the way; it's here right now. It as simple as four little words: *Jesus, I accept you.* If you will stop right now and repeat that statement, I am prepared to show you how to leave all this behind you and get what my baby girl calls a "daddy do-over." What I am trying to say is that by accepting Christ into your life, you will allow a change to occur—a change that will affect your whole life.

Let's try a little exercise. Picture someone in your life whom you love. It may be your mom, your dad, your sister, your brother—just someone who meets a few qualifications for this exercise to work. This person has to have been there through all of your drama, whether it be bailing you out of jail, crying over you, having money stolen by you, or being lied to daily. And this person must be someone you love more than anything. Imagine that person sitting there, anxiously, night after night, worrying about whether you're alive, if you have overdosed, or if you have killed someone or been killed in a drug deal gone bad. Imagine how that person must feel. But his or her feelings cannot compare to one tenth of the grief you have caused your father in heaven. The tears you have made him shed for the choices you have made are numerous. Think about how excited he must be when you say, "God, I give it all to you"—and then you take it back, kind of like that special person you have let down so many times. Here is the secret: that person you were thinking of can't do anything more than feel for you. God, on the other hand, has already healed you.

Imagine finding the cure for cancer. Would you tell everyone about it? That is what I'm telling you right now—you have found the cure for the cancer in your life. You have found the cure for addiction: this program. Share it. During my time as an addict, I can't begin to tell you how many times I thought, *This is real. I can do it*. But in no time I would pick up the phone and buy another gram of dope. If you will give everything over to God, step back, stop, and let God be God—oh my, what lies ahead of you. It is critical that you understand how this step is done, so I will show you.

Simply say, "God, I come before you to ask for help. I know you're real, and you are the same god that created me and this earth. Therefore, I give up my will to use drugs and lay it at your feet for you to help me with. I ask for your help in the name of Jesus Christ, amen." And there it is—that's how to give something up.

# Chapter 5

## Step Four: Don't Take It Back

Unlike the other chapters, this one will be very short. There is only so much that can be said about not taking back what you have given to God. You may believe, as I did, that you have given it all over to God more times than you can count, but have you really? This step involves relying on facts, scriptures, and references to help you avoid taking back something that you have given to God. No matter how bad of a day you might be having or on which road you are traveling, under no circumstances can you skip this step. Doing so will open the door for a relapse. Here is an example.

I'm blessed to own a successful automotive business, and my will is to always stay focused and to make money. God's will, however, is for me to give back and to help people in the community. When I overlook his will, his blessings tighten up, both emotionally and financially, and nothing gets accomplished. A woman came into my store one day in need of a major repair that would cost over two thousand dollars and a minor repair priced at over three hundred dollars. I had this feeling that I needed to help. She could afford only the major repair. After talking with my wife and praying, we decided to do the minor repair at no cost.

When the customer came to pick up her vehicle and realized that both the major and the minor repairs were done, she began to weep. You see, the minor repair was on her front and rear brakes; if left unaddressed, they could have become a danger. Not being able to stop your car could be life threatening. As she was weeping, she began to explain to me that she had been ready to give up on

God. She said she had spoken to God and told him that she needed a miracle, and lo and behold that miracle was given through the grace of God. As for my wife and me, we were blessed tenfold.

I am not sharing these stories with you to imply that you should give this kind of gift. I just want to show you that, finally, for the first time in my life, I am being part of the solution instead of the problem. I am also pleading with you to allow God the necessary time to work these miracles in your life. We have become a drive-through society, a hurry-up, can't-sit-down kind of people. That's why I say, "Stop!" There is nothing in this world more important right now than your being where you are, doing what you're doing, reading what you're reading. I don't want to sound like a motivational guru or a salesman; rather, I need you to feel something that you have never felt by the end of this book.

I remember when I was living in my pickup truck and thinking, *My God, this can't get any worse.* Sure enough, it did. I then lost my truck and went to living underneath an overpass two blocks away from the million dollar home I had lost some two years earlier.

So I hope you understand that once you give it all over, you should leave it there and not take it back. In this life, we are tested, and after we allow God into our lives, we may be tested specifically to see if our faith is strong enough to let all of our problems stay at God's feet. Certain scriptures may help you become as madly in love with God as David was; see Psalms 5, Psalms 9, Psalms 20, Psalms 51, and Psalms 34:7-22. These scriptures are all examples of how God took over all of David's worries and allowed him victory over all his fears.

# Chapter 6

## Step Five: Expect the Miracle

When I tell people that I had never seen drugs until I was in my late twenties, it blows their minds that I could have fallen so far so fast. In the fall of 1994, I was studying for my state general contractor license in Utah and was at a local equipment rental company when, out of the blue, the clerk looked at me and said, "You seem exhausted." I proceeded to explain that I had been up most of the night studying and was at the end of my rope. I will never forget what she said then: "Listen, I have something that will not only keep you awake; it will make you feel like Superman!" I was, to say the least, a little confused but simply said, "Hell, I'll try anything once."

Let me take a moment to explain something to you. I had never in my life depended on alcohol or any type of drug until I took painkillers. But Satan wants people like me and like you. A belief that Satan is real comes with your belief that God is real. We know that Satan was placed here on this earth to tempt us. He will not be satisfied until he has you; only then will his temptation stop. I am here to tell you that nothing of this world can beat addiction; the cure has to come from out of this world.

It is also very important to know that Satan will identify himself just like God tries to identify himself to you, in the smallest, simplest ways. He will use family, friends, coworkers, strangers—anyone and anything—just to get you down. He will use these people to influence you and make you feel depressed. He can make a feeling of being overwhelmed come over you. It is my belief that Satan will also use the things of this world, like money, power, and so on, to harm you and make you fall, but drugs are his most powerful temptation. It's no different from when he tempted Eve in the Garden of Eden. His use of drugs is simply his favorite temptation. For you, it's the apple of this dispensation.

After trying meth for the first time in 1994, I spent the next ten years chasing a repeat of that first high. That feeling you get the first time you get high is one you chase continually until you die, go to prison for life, or beat it. Those are the three choices you're faced with once you have become an addict. It is unlike anything you have ever known. It grabs you slowly and doesn't like to let go of you at all. I don't know many people who have successfully become sober after being addicted to meth.

In my opinion, I was a pretty functional addict at first, or at least I thought I was at the time. It would seem to someone who had never been exposed to drugs that I was normal but a little high strung. I would shoot up in the morning and use at night, but I never did either around the kids and never at home. As my addiction increased, so did my usage. I had two children and a good wife when my addiction started and wound up with four more children by three other wives within the next five years.

I owned a very successful asphalt company from 1989 until 1998, lived in a ten thousand square foot home, and had a live-in nanny. I had everything that one could ask for, it would seem, but in reality, I had nothing. I know that faith is very important to have, but looking back, I see that I had lost all faith in everything—myself, my relationships, everything. My very ability to function as a man was gone. I had lost all hope, which in turn took me deeper into my addiction. My usage increased, and the quality of my life decreased. This is that vicious cycle I keep referring to. I began to attract new friends who would help me during my downfall but would in fact cost me everything yet again. I can't seem to find the words to tell you just how quickly Satan and this addiction take over your life.

Many books will tell you that meth releases serotonin, which is what makes you feel happy, what gives you that natural high. But I cannot name five people who have successfully stopped using. I set out to write down what finally worked for me, how throughout my struggles I have gained strength from each and every test I have been through. That's how these steps came to be; it's like God wanted it to be so simple that even a baby could get it—a baby like me.

I went into and out of every kind of program known to man throughout my addiction years, all to no avail. I went to daily programs as well as outpatient programs (too many to count), even programs while in prison or county jail. I had tried to follow God twice before in my life only to come up with nail-biting sobriety that would last a few days or more. Even with all the effort, nothing fit me. I could always find some great reason to go out and get wasted.

The first time I spent any length of time in a Utah correctional facility was the first time I met Jim. I had been running and gunning for over six years straight and had not had any real trouble with the law until my money ran out and I crossed that forbidden line between customer and retailer (addict to dealer). I had a successful company and lived in a huge home, but eventually it all caught up to me. There were not enough drugs in the world to fill the hole I was trying to fill.

Now that I am looking back, what seems so strange to me is that, to this day, I cannot tell you what that hole was. All I know is that it was deep and scary, and I didn't dare slow down long enough to take a look inside of myself to see what was there. When you have crossed over to the dealer side, the whole game changes. You have taken a step that makes it hard to ever feel anything again. Once, I did some work for a cop in town and knew that he liked weed and pills. We went to the same Mormon church. I asked him if he was interested in making a little money, and he said he was. Now what I am about to tell you is not fake. It's as real as everything I have told you already, but you may think it sounds too much like the movies. It's not from a script, though. This really happened.

I asked my cop friend what officers did if they were first on the scene and found money and drugs. He told me their procedure, and bells were going off in my head. We began a joint business deal that would eventually land me in jail and get him suspended from the force. When the cops made a bust, he would give me the money they found, and I would buy dope with it, sell the dope, and split the profit down the middle. It all went fine until he began to use with me. It progressed to the point that I would take all the drugs from the busts as well as the money, and he would call for back up and report that no drugs or money had been found. It was smooth sailing. I was selling drugs to the cops and getting my dope for free—until his first dirty drug test. Then all hell broke loose.

If you were to ask yourself, "Does God love me?" would you answer, "Yes, he does"? What makes King David of the Old Testament more special than you? The answer can be summarized in one simple word—nothing. I have six children, and I love them all the same. No matter what they might do individually, it won't make me love that one more than another. In the same way, God loves us all equally. The only variable is how much we love him. That is why great things were done through David.

I began to have run-ins with the law only after I stopped working so hard and was no longer making the money necessary to maintain the high I needed each and every single day. My then wife and I had a habit that cost in excess of three hundred dollars per day. It seemed like all we ever did was get high. It was also at this time that we began shooting up. That would take things to a whole new level, one I had never dreamed of.

I remember living in a million dollar home but using a generator in the garage for power. It was awful. My habit was so expensive that I couldn't even pay the light bill. I guess you could say I was destined to fall; it was only a matter of time. We had an expensive habit, and I did whatever it took to get and maintain my high. Once I began to deal drugs, I entered a world that made just using drugs seem like a walk in the park. Dealing is like a whole new addiction. It's a high in itself because you feel like you're invincible.

As a child, I had regular dreams just like you did—dreams of being a fireman, a doctor, or a lawyer. I wanted everything everyone else wanted. I never dreamed I would become a drug addict, let alone a dealer. It caught me by surprise. It happened so quietly, and before I knew it, I was all the way in. It's almost like becoming part of an organized crime family: once you're in, it's hard to get out.

Unlike any other program, this five-step program is not going to ask you to take any moral inventories or to make amends with those whom you have offended. You will have to believe that your higher power is God. The goal of these five steps is to help you create a relationship with God that is so powerful, so mighty, and so amazing that nothing of this world or in this world can destroy it. That's the whole key: what you're doing is much bigger than this world or this life you're dealing with. It goes beyond that. It's your soul the devil wants; he aims to interfere with your salvation. Once you begin your walk and start taking your steps, I ask you to honestly believe that you're completely healed. Jesus has paid for your sins and has and will make all the amends necessary to regain the relationships that became infected as a result of your actions while in your addiction. Notice I said *infected*, not *affected*. You have to look at this as a disease that Satan himself uses on God's children, something that he can destroy lives with, something that is so powerful that it can consume you until you die. It can literally take your soul to death and hell. What is beautiful about it all, though, is that you have the choice to allow Christ in. I know it's hard, but you're still free to make your choices in life. Being an addict is like having cancer: you can survive it if you get the help needed. The dope can take your freedom and, yes, even your life, but it can't take what is important—your inner self, your core. You must try to take it one day at time.

For the past fifteen years, I have spent every day of every week trying to find out why I'm an addict, why I blew what I blew, why I destroyed whom I destroyed, and why I lost what I lost. I've asked myself if it was my childhood, if it was because my dad was an alcoholic, or if was related to the friends I kept only to realize that it was none of these things, nor was it a chemical imbalance. It was the choices I made while simultaneously allowing a breakdown in my belief in God and the lack of a relationship with him. I allowed Satan to enter my life by using drugs. Try to remember the best drugs you've ever done—I am not talking good but the best ever—the highest you've ever been, the most money you've ever made, and the best you've ever looked. All of this combined times three cannot equal the feeling of a day-to-day, intimate relationship with God that includes the pure knowledge that he's there with you every single step you take in a day.

I know some readers will think, *This guy is out there*. If you're one of them, put the book down, and then, when you're at the end of your rope and reach rock bottom, pick it back up and this will be right here waiting for you. But I want you to know that as real as the words you are reading now are, so are the words that will come to you from God if you will do the five steps outlined. Actually expect the miracle that awaits you.

If your doctor told you that if you didn't take certain pills every day you would surely die, you would take the pills. That same principle applies to your addiction. If you don't do these five steps, you're going to die. In other words, stop doing what you're doing now and start doing what you need to do now:

Step 1: Identify your god.
Step 2: Pray without ceasing.
Step 3: Give it all to God.
Step 4: Don't take it back.
Step 5: Expect the miracle.

I can remember times when I would get clean but the dreams I would have would always make me want to get high. You know what I am talking about—having dreams about using and waking up in cold sweats. I'm here to tell you that now, I have zero memory of how it felt to be high, zero dreams, and zero desire to use drugs whatsoever. Those have physically been taken from me. Christ has actually removed all my physical desire to use drugs. In the course of my day, I go through the five steps too many times to count. I wake up every day identifying my god by saying my morning prayer, and I pray without ceasing throughout the entire day until I retire at night. I will get with my wife at work several times a day and pray with her. I give my day over to God for his will to be done. Once I've done that, I don't take it back.

Finally, the step that is probably the most difficult is expecting the miracle to be done. In my case, doing these steps has allowed me to become closer than ever before to Christ both mentally and in my heart—so close that I actually feel him. Did you understand what I said? I'm so close to God sometimes that I can actually feel his presence. Each and every day I expect every single prayer I pray to become true. Pretty bold, isn't it—expecting God to answer every single one of my prayers? The last time I checked, the god I worshiped is a pretty bold god.

Therapists have said that a person has to be ready to quit drugs before he or she can quit them, that he or she has to reach rock bottom before any program will work. Well, in my opinion, that's bull crap. No matter what stage of your addiction you're in—beginning, middle, or end—God is anxiously waiting to hear your cry for help. I hope that you can understand what I'm trying to relay to you. What I'm trying to say and what I pray that my words help explain to you is that you can be cured right now. If you were diagnosed tonight, God forbid, with a form of terminal cancer, what would you do tonight? Think before you answer: what would you actually do? Would you cry to God? What would you do right this second? Take just a moment and imagine what you would do. Now, with that same intensity is the way you have to look at what addiction is. You have to look at your situation as if you don't have another chance coming tomorrow, as if death were here. Right now, no other choices can be available if you're going to make it. It's as if your life depends on your making the right choice right now. Nothing in this life can or will be more important than the relationship with your heavenly father that awaits you right here and right now.

My first meltdown happened in the winter of 2000. I had just gotten released from the county jail in Utah after doing the most time I had had to do up until that point in my life—thirty days. I was facing a lot more time, though. I knew that I would be convicted on some of the charges filed. The first-degree felony for distribution of a controlled substance times three, meaning three counts, carried a five-year to life sentence in the state of Utah, in addition to two counts of possession, which carried a one-year to fifteen-year sentence. My mom was pretty sick at the time, dying from diabetes, and I needed, or wanted, to head home to Florida. I hadn't been back home in a very long time, and since I had been born and raised in Florida, I missed it. I had just completed my thirty-day visit at the "hard rock hotel" (county) and was out on a one hundred thousand dollar bond for the five charges and decided I was going to my mom's. She had recently moved to Alabama, though, to be closer to a bigger hospital than the one in Bonifay, Florida. I left, and I could then add to my record "fugitive from justice." When you're out on bond or bail, you are not permitted to leave the area, let alone the entire state. But there I was, leaving Utah. It makes sense now as I look back. At the time, I was focused on me, me, me, I want, I want, I want. I didn't realize how serious that charge was, nor did I realize that I would have federal marshals on my trail. I didn't care. I wanted to see my mom, and I knew she was not going to make it much longer.

I arrived in Dothan, Alabama, to find my mother on dialysis two times a week. One of the hardest things I've had to do is watch someone die when I was in the military. But without a doubt, the hardest thing I've ever had to do was watch my mother drown to death because she stopped her dialysis treatments. I started using again, and believe it or not, my actions again left me untouchable to both my emotions and my family. It was a very sad time in my life, but to my surprise my addiction worsened.

It happened so fast. All of a sudden, Mom decided she was done with dialysis. One day, I was taking her to her twice-weekly appointment, and she wouldn't get out of the car. She said, "I want to go fishing." I explained that there was no way on this earth that I could take her, and then she said in a firmer voice, almost demanding, "I want to go fishing . . . please." I continued to argue until she looked at me with the most peaceful eyes I had ever seen, grabbed my arm, and repeated, "I want to go fishing."

I called the doctor in, and we began coming to the decision that it was time for Mom to stop fighting and get ready to die. I can't explain it, but even as I am writing this, it makes me choke up with tears—thinking about her and all the memories around her and her time here on this earth. Knowing she would be dead in only a matter of days really brought back memories, like the first time that I actually saw snow and how she took me out of school and we played in it all day. I couldn't have been more than six years old. I remember that no matter how bad of a day I was having, I could always count on that smile, a hug, and a kiss. I will never forget going to the Piggly Wiggly and begging her for breakfast cereal. She would give in, and I would have to sneak it the house because we were always big breakfast eaters in my home and cereal generally wasn't allowed. When you come from an abusive home where your father is a binge drinker and does nothing but beat you, you grow really close to your mom. I was a complete mama's boy and proud of it.

My mother did all she could to help me avoid becoming the man that I was becoming up to that point prior to her death. Right then, I was not feeling anything at all due to how high I was. I was so messed up that I was unable to mourn the impending death of the greatest mother in the world. But what blows my mind is that I wasn't even at the bottom yet. I actually dug my hole deeper than it had ever been before.

So with the decision made, we loaded up and drove to the store, where I bought her an RC Cola and a MoonPie, and we went fishing. I drove her to a park with a lake where I don't even think fishing is allowed, but we did anyway. It was like old times. As a child, my mother would take me on regular fishing outings to Lake Victor. She would haul a number 5 washtub down to the pier so that she could fill it with water, and then she would throw the fish she caught into the tub for me. I would spend the entire day fishing with my toy reel and rod. I recalled times like these as the days leading toward the end of my mom's life progressed, the toxins in her blood making her go in and out of sanity.

I remember one time in particular when she asked me to sit down and said that she needed me to give her the baby that then wife number four was carrying (unbeknownst to either of us). To placate her, I told her that she could have him, but she persisted so much that I had to go to the local Kmart and buy a baby doll. I gave it to her, and as she held it, she would occasionally look up at me and say, "You think I'm crazy, don't you?" Then she would turn back to the doll and say, "Aww, don't worry, baby. Granny got you. Everything will be all right, I promise."

It was four days later at around two o'clock in the morning that my mother died with that baby doll in her arms. I had stayed up for three days straight, and they turned out to be the last three days of her life. I was told she had slipped into a coma and that it would be only a matter of hours, but three days later she was still with us. It was then that the hospice nurse came in, looked me in the eye, and said, "Let her go." I said, "What do you mean?" She said, "She won't die because you won't let her. I have something to help you sleep." She handed me a pill, and after I took it, I leaned over and tearfully said, "Mommy, I am going to be all right. You can go now. Please know I will always love you." I stood up and went to the couch, and twenty minutes later I heard screaming. I knew she had died. I ran to her and heard her gurgling. I screamed, "She is not dead!" The nurse told me that what I heard was the sound of the fluid around her heart releasing. It's a sound I'll never forget.

It's almost as if she knew my wife and I were going to have a baby and that she needed to protect it from harm. She knew that I was not done using; in fact, my darkest days were just ahead of me. I've always heard that people who are getting ready to go back to God experience something special. I could see that in my mom's eyes. It's as close as a person can come to Christ while still here on this earth. Despite all this, the deep end of my addiction got a little deeper.

I have always looked for reasons to mess up my life. I am one of those people who will mess up a great thing just because I'm sure it's only a matter of time before it gets messed up anyway. It's not an intentional thing; it's just more addictive behavior I have had to learn to outgrow. I look back and realize that Mom's death was, to say the least, the turning point in my recovery. I didn't know it then, but it put me on the right course to get straight.

I was almost incapable of feelings at that point in my life. A person's normal life span once dialysis is stopped is no more than three days, but my mother held on for more than ten days. Her love for me was truly unconditional. As for my wife at the time, I stayed with her for three more months and then sent her back to Utah, not knowing I had a son on the way.

By then, I was getting close to the end of my freedom or to my death. I went from general using to the worst thing possible: mixing meth with cocaine. I can remember doing shots so big that I would almost die, and then I would look up toward heaven and laugh because I hadn't. Because I have been that low, I truly know that you can, without a doubt, beat any addiction you're dealing with at any time and withstand any situation you're in no matter what. I'm telling you that God is, to put it simply, ready to rescue you from the deepest hole, the darkest cave, and the worst condition you have ever been in. That's when God shines the brightest. He is anxiously waiting for those three simple words to be said: "God, I surrender."

After my mom's death, the responsibility of taking care of the old man fell to me. My father is a very good man in his own way, but he was not much of a father. In fact, what he taught me was how *not* to be a father. It is very important that you know that he and his actions toward me did not make me become an addict. However, it took me more than twenty-five years to realize, believe, and say that. We have to take full responsibility for our addictions and behaviors.

I remember that when I was in sixth grade, my mom took a job at the school across the street from our house so that we wouldn't be home when Dad would return after a week-long drunk. My dad was what you would call a binge drinker; whether he had one beer or one hundred didn't matter because he knew he would get in the same amount of trouble once he got home. He would do great for months at a time, and then out of the blue he would be gone for weeks. I also believe that my mom took the custodian job partly to ensure that we had money for food when Dad was gone for long periods of time.

As I said earlier, my mom's side of the family was amazing, but my dad's side was rather distant. As a result, my dad was an extremely abusive alcoholic. One time that really sticks out in my mind is when I was maybe eight years old and my mom's appendix burst while Dad was on a binge. He showed up at the hospital to take me home and then left for a week. I was found in the closet severely dehydrated and sitting in my own feces. See, in my house, kids were required to ask for permission to go to the refrigerator. I was so afraid that if I tried to get a drink or some food, Dad would show up while I was doing so and the beating would be awful. My father stood six feet tall and weighed over two hundred fifty pounds. When he would beat my siblings and me, he swung that belt until he got tired. Every single time that I was beaten, I bled.

Then, for my tenth birthday, I wanted a BMX racer bicycle. The local Western Auto had one for ninety-nine dollars, which, back in the seventies, was like a thousand dollars nowadays. I found out that my mom had saved up and was getting me one, so I let the cat out of the bag. I just had to tell everyone that I was having a birthday party, so all my friends were planning to come over. That excitement that a child gets when he really wants something and will even be the first to get it is powerful. Well, somehow, Dad had gotten the money from Mom several days earlier and had gone on a binge with it. Mom started acting very strangely; she obviously didn't have a back-up plan. You guessed it: there was no bike at my birthday party. Instead, I got a white goat. I was, to say the least, so humiliated that some damage was done.

I continued to grow up as normally as anyone and was somehow able to avoid the pitfalls of drugs until I was out of my teens. So even though I was subjected to both mental and physical abuse, I can still say that my father did not make me an addict. It was my choice only. I had the chance, and I chose to become what I became. To this day, I credit my sister with saving my life simply because she always knew when and where to come to either save me or pick me up.

In my opinion, drug addiction is the worst epidemic in our country today, tearing up our children, our husbands, and our families. We are anxiously seeking a cure for AIDS. We are spending billions upon billions of dollars searching for the cure for cancer, but a lot of them stem from some form of addiction. In an informal survey that a corrections officer and I conducted at a local jail, 90 percent of the inmates were convicted on drug-related charges. Take a minute to think about what I am telling you. Drug addiction is the single most dangerous disease known to man. It is without a doubt the most commonly used and most successful tool of the devil.

If you are not an addict but are reading this book in hopes of helping someone who is, then I want to make this bold proclamation to you: if you do these five steps and turn over that person like he would turn over his addiction to God, I promise you in the name of Jesus Christ that you will be made whole and he will be healed. Addicts never take anyone's thoughts and feelings into consideration. In fact, there's no job, no home, no child, no sibling, no parent, no anything that comes before getting their drugs. They are so caught up in their lifestyles that they are completely incapable of compassion. If you are an addict, I want to encourage you to put the book down, get on your knees, and pray. If you've never prayed before, just say something simple, like, "God, here I am. Help me, please. I'm sick. Help me, please. In Jesus' name, amen." Then sit there and be quiet, listening to your thoughts as they run through your mind. Try to allow your mind to be open and inviting to what lies ahead. Think about the happiest times of your life. What were they? I'd almost be willing to bet you that they had something to do with your family or a brush with God.

One of my favorite books was written by Michael D. Evans. It's called *The Prayer of David: In Times of Trouble*, and one of my favorite parts says, "Help is on the way! No matter what you're going through emotionally, physically, financially, socially, legally, help is on the way, if you will but put your trust in God's power. God really does understand where we are in our situations, circumstances and trials. He sees our black holes of poverty, grief, abuse, neglect, unhappiness, malaise in life. Yes, help is on the way. All that is needed is to just get the flesh out of the way so God can show up—big time."

The flesh gets in the way. If that doesn't make sense, then let me explain a little more. I believe, as do most followers of Christ, that we as humans are made of flesh and bones but that we also have an inner spirit that is made in the likeness of God. The Bible tells us this, so when I say the flesh gets in the way, I mean it literally gets in the way. We as children of God have a core or spirit that wants to be good, wants to do good, wants to please God, and—yes, believe it or not—wants to be as pure as the driven snow. It is not easy to do because we (our flesh) crave the things of this world. It can become addicted so easily because it feels those things so well. That is why I have made every attempt to show you that I couldn't stop using drugs on my own. I had to have divine intervention to stop using. I found myself broken, with nothing left but my spirit, and yet I would fail time and time again. So how did I make it happen? I sought out a personal relationship with my maker, and once it was in place, I accepted this huge gift from Christ. I actually accepted him as savior and allowed his death to pay for my sins. That's right—Christ's blood has paid for my addiction and everything I have ever done or will do.

But that's another book. Working through the five simple steps every day is not rocket science at all. In fact, it's so simple because that's the way God intends it to be. Just as penicillin was discovered to be a treatment for infection, I have found the cure for addiction. Is faith required? Why, yes, it is. So shall I define *faith* for you? That can be done with this simple question: have you ever seen a million dollars in cash in front of you? If your answer is no, then I ask you, is it possible for you to make a million dollars? If your answer is yes, then you have faith. If God created and loved the world, then why couldn't he love you enough to cure you and heal you right now? Is it going to be easy? Absolutely not. Anything of worth in life is never easy.

There will be times when you will feel alone and like you have the weight of the world on you. That's when you will, without a doubt, have to work through these five steps daily. When you are at your weakest is when you will need that personal relationship. In the Bible, Job didn't have a clue that the end of his life would be better than it had been before God tested him. God eventually restored everything that Job had lost and then some. I promise you that relationships will be restored and that you will be blessed financially. You can do things better than you have ever done before. I'm talking riches that cannot be measured. It's almost like a domino effect. During my addiction, I gave up and prayed for death more times than I can count. Now that I have been on life support and had my heart in the hands of a cardiologist for more than nine hours, I don't pray that anymore. In fact, I catch myself feeling grateful and excited at the beginning of each and every new day.

If you have given up on life, please don't allow death to occupy your precious thoughts anymore. I beg you to read and reread this book and follow its steps, and your life will change. I have prayed without ceasing for God to convey everything I intend in my writing in hopes that you too can be saved and not die from what you're doing.

I never understood what my addiction did to my parents until just recently. I was in church, and the preacher was giving a powerful sermon. The spirit of the Lord was in the house. My dear friend was next to me; I knew that his son had just been arrested for the second time on drug-related charges, and I could feel his pain. I turned to him and hugged him, and we began to weep. He said, "What did I do wrong, and what do I do now?" As we wept, I told him how blessed he was that his son was in jail. I explained, "At least he is not high." Then I told him that nothing in this world he had done had anything to do with his son's choices—nothing at all. I then grabbed his hand and rubbed it along the scar from the incision for my open-heart surgery. I said, "At least he's still young enough that if he stops, he won't have the health problems I have now." We continued to share and pray. I prayed, "Thank you for this friend of mine. Let him know that he's not to blame and, God, may he find joy and peace from this experience."

It's easy now to write these words because of where I am in my life, but it wasn't easy getting here. I promise you that these five simple steps will work for you:

1.  Identify your god.
2.  Pray without ceasing.
3.  Give it all to God.
4.  Don't take it back.
5.  Expect the miracle.

They are truly inspired. The reason I listed them again is that I want to emphasize just how simple they are. Nothing could be simpler than working through these steps. One of the biggest problems I had time and time again when going to meetings for other programs was all the steps. How could I ever make amends to all I have offended? It just seemed to be overwhelming. When I set out to write down what worked for me, I prayed for the Lord to show me how to convey it in the least number of words possible.

# I Surrender, God

Three simple words will define the rest of your life from this point forward: "I surrender, God." If these words are spoken with real intent, they will, without a doubt, change your life. What a powerful statement it can be. Once spoken, it sends out an invitation to the most powerful being to enter into your life. It opens the door to allow him in to take over your life to the point that he can guide you through struggles and toward greater happiness.

I must ask you a simple question: do you truly know what it means to surrender your will to God? Do you or can you begin to understand what it means to become completely submissive to your god to the point that all you do in your life is his will? It is not an easy task, but it is the most rewarding one a person can do in this life.

As you read the Bible, you will encounter stories from cover to cover of how kings and leaders and just plain ordinary people surrendered to God daily. It tells you how they were tested and how they were rewarded. But most of all, it tells you of an unexplainable love that God gives to you for this surrendering that you do. The Bible is full of these stories, such as Jesus healing the blind, the sick, the drunk, and the prostitute. So why would our times be any different? Surrendering your will means you will become totally submissive to God's will and are willing to do anything asked of you by God.

Do you think that God can communicate with you? No, really. Do you think he will actually take the time to talk to you and reveal his will to you? Well, my friend, the answer to that question is simple—yes. Do you talk to your children? Do you talk to your earthly father? I am here to testify that God wants such a real relationship with you that he will show you everything needed to get you through this life until you meet him again. He will lead people into your life who will help you get where you need to be. He will come to you in your dreams. If there is a secret that we were sent to earth to discover, then this would be it: how well we can surrender our will to God. There. It's out of the bag. The secret has been told.

Perhaps you have heard the story of Abraham and his son Isaac from Genesis 22. God promised that Abraham would be a father of many nations. In fact, he would have more descendants than there were grains of sand upon the sea shore. Well, after reaching a ripe age somewhere in his late eighties to early nineties, he was still childless. Finally, God blessed him with a son. Can you begin to imagine how happy Abraham must have been? But God decided to test Abraham by telling him to go to the altar and sacrifice his only son in God's honor. Despite the fact that Abraham must have felt like dying, he never doubted God whatsoever. In other words, he was will-less before his god. He began to carry out God's will, but right before he could kill his son, God stopped him. Abraham looked over at the tree line and saw a ram tangled in a bush; God had provided it for the sacrifice instead. That's the kind of determination you have to take on today in order to fulfill your destiny. If you want to make it and survive this addiction, you have no choice in the matter. God has to lead your life 100 percent. If you cannot accept this practice, then you must set the book down because you will not get it. Something happened to me recently when I was dealing with an addict who just didn't get it. He had a job that paid him six figures and a beautiful woman in his life, and he had put together two weeks of sobriety. He didn't know who God is, so I proceeded to introduce these five steps to him. As we were talking, I told him that not using is easy; it's all the other crap that goes with it that gets hard. I encouraged him to go to his room, kneel, and say, "God, I don't know if you're real or not. Jay has told me you are. And God, all I can say is help me. I surrender." Well, no lights shone down from heaven, but one thing did happen: he at least got on his knees.

Will he stay sober? Is he healed? I can't answer those questions yet, but I can tell you that what he was doing wasn't working. What he did that day got him through it sober. Each person has a different story. In fact, that's one of the problems. All addicts think that they are not like anyone else, that their addiction is worse than anybody else's has ever been. I am here to tell you that that's bull crap. That's a plain and simple thinking error. I titled this book *I Surrender All* because it's the entire point of our lives here on this earth. I would like to try to help you understand what you're surrendering to God.

If you fix a cup of coffee after you wake up in the morning, you don't have to stop doing that. That's not the kind of surrendering I am talking about. If someone cuts you off while you're driving and you want to flip him off, opting not to is surrendering. If you want to buy a new four wheeler but don't because your family needs new clothes, that's surrendering. Remember the steps:

1. Identify your god.
2. Pray without ceasing.
3. Give it all to God.
4. Don't take it back.
5. Expect the miracle.

I start my day out by saying in my morning prayers, "God, help me surrender my will, and let your will be done in my life today." It's very important that you be able to identify God's will in your life on a day-to-day basis. There are so many ways you can do this, but the main thing to remember is that if it doesn't feel right, then it probably isn't.

The first thing we can do is start a study program of his word, the Bible. Even if you read only one chapter a day, at least you're trying it. Another way is by asking him to reveal his will to you and allowing him to show you that will. You can begin doing his will by living a better life than you have been and by being kinder to your wife, your friends, and your neighbors.

Living by the Ten Commandments is another way of showing God that you want his will in your life. However, I think it goes a lot further than that. I believe that we are asked to go the extra mile, and by that I mean help others who are where we used to be. We can agree that we are saved by grace, which is a gift no one can take from us. God has given it freely to us. We must take that love and help others recognize the fact that they too are saved and can rejoice in that knowledge.

I promised myself when I set out to write this book that I would make it less about me and more about God, but as I write it I can't help but notice how lost I was for so many years and how I couldn't grasp this concept completely. Unless you are at a point in your life where nothing else matters but being healed—not getting sober, but being healed so that it's gone forever—then you're in for trouble. Put yourself in a position where you can't fail by praying all the time. I remember being fresh on the streets with over two years of clean time under my belt since I had been behind bars, and I remember how I truly did not want to mess it up. Then, in less than sixty days, I was right back where I had been. Programs didn't work for me. Advice from people telling me over and over and over again what to do went in one ear and out the other. Then I got into a halfway house, and the judge told me, "Son, if you don't complete this program successfully, I will lock you up and throw away the key. You will do a five-year to life sentence." And after six months, I ran. Can you believe that, even with that over my head, I still couldn't give up the dope? So how did I finally do it? I surrendered all to God!

In the New Testament, Ephesians 4:25-32 (New Living Translation) says:

> So stop telling lies. Let us tell our neighbors the truth, for we are all parts of the same body. And don't sin by letting your anger control you. Don't let the sun go down while you're still angry, for anger gives a foot-hold to the devil. If you're a thief, quit stealing, instead use your hands for good hard work, and then give generously to others in need. Don't use foul or abusive language. Let everything you say be good and helpful, so that your words will be an encouragement to those who hear them. And do not bring sorrow to God's holy spirit by the way you live. Remember, he has identified you as his own, guaranteeing that you will be saved on the day of redemption. Get rid of all bitterness, rage, anger, harsh words, and slander, as well as all types of evil behavior. Instead, be kind to each other, tenderhearted, forgiving one another, just as God through Christ has forgiven you.

If that doesn't show you God's will, then I don't know what else to say.

So as you have read, surrendering can take many forms and can, if done properly, make you a better person. I want you to understand that if you will give up your will to God, you will show him how faithful you are trying to become. Our will is the greatest gift we can give him. If we turn over everything, we and everything we do has God involved. We may still make some mistakes as we're learning, but the chances that we will get high or drunk will be greatly diminished.

# Chapter 7

## Kaylee's Song

I hope you can bear with me for a few pages as I attempt to explain why I am still, to this day, going through recovery as an addict. Using my own experiences, I am going to show you that these steps will and do work. On December 26, 2010, I had just hung up the phone with my estranged eighteen-year-old daughter. I have missed every single Christmas since she was ten years old. I remember the day she was born into this world. Oh my, was I a proud papa. Something about that firstborn ensures that no one else can ever take her place. I guess it's the newness of parenthood. I had not yet begun using drugs and was so proud to be a dad. I remember rubbing her mom's tummy and singing to her every single night for nine months. She was Daddy's little girl. With that in mind, you can understand how I have suffered so much by not having her in my life for all these years. I have prayed and given it over to God more times than anyone can count only to take it back and then screw it up.

That day in December was like all the other times before, if not worse. I threw my will and not God's will into play. I was so hell-bent on being the recovered dad and determined that I was not going to miss another Christmas. Well, it backfired in my face. So this is an example of how you go through the five steps. The only difference is that I applied them to my relationship with my daughter instead of to my addiction that time. I prayed, "God I know who you are and how much a part of my life you are each and every day. I have, without a doubt, prayed to you for years concerning my daughter

Kaylee. God, at this time in my life, I give her to you to protect, to watch after, and most important to provide for her each day. Give her strength in her body to do your will. Now, God, I make this promise to you, that I will not take it back. My will is your will, and Father, if it's your will that I never speak to her again, I will accept this. I won't like it, but I will accept it. I promise this to you, God. I have caused more pain than she, at this time in her life, is willing to forgive me for, and God, for this I am so sorry. But, Father, you have made me whole again and freed me from the bondage of drugs and all the behaviors that come with that life, so I believe in you, God. I believe that you're the same god of Moses, who parted the Red Sea, and I know that same power is at my call. Therefore, I call upon you, God, to take this in your arms at this time and make it whole. I do this in Jesus' name, amen."

Now that I have prayed my prayer, I have covered the first four steps and am now waiting for that miracle to happen. I want you to see that it's true that miracles do happen, so let me share what happened to me on the most recent Father's Day. It was late that afternoon, and out of the blue Kaylee texted me with, "I have never really said happy Father's Day to anyone except my grandpa once, but I really want you to have a happy Father's Day from me." I'm telling you that if the end of time were to be today, it would not shock me more or make me more happy. I am so excited to be on the right track again with her. Don't ever give up on your relationships.

# Chapter 8

## Fixing My Broken Heart

I will never forget the first time I laid my eyes on my sweetheart. It was in March, and I was in a reentry program. I was heading to church and, wouldn't you know it, God once again showed up when I least expected it. I had never met the family that was picking me up to take me to church. Remember, I was still waiting to be sentenced on the charges from years ago, so this reentry program was run through the county jail. One of the mentors arrived to pick me up, and in the front seat of the van was the most beautiful angel I had ever seen in my entire life. Her name was Katie.

I introduced myself to her and got into the van to go to church. I can remember the hope that her handshake gave me, as well the peace I felt every time she would speak. I wasn't looking for love, let alone God, in the van that day. But he revealed himself, and both were born. I became very close to the mentor, Katie's mom, and found myself listening to and hanging onto every piece of advice she would give me. I also became very close friends with Katie, and a relationship in Christ was born. Allow me to shed some light on this for a minute. I had never been in any type of relationship in which sex, drugs, or money wasn't the major part, so for the first time I was actually involved with someone I wasn't sleeping with or doing drugs with. And for the first time I was actually falling in love for all the right reasons. I remember asking God to, one day, if it be his will, bless me with someone just like Katie. He did on August 13, 2009, the day we were married, and with her support I made it through a near-death experience.

I had, in my mind, reached and was finally on the course that God would have me on, and then only six weeks into the program I had a mild heart attack. Prior to that, I had begun a relationship with God that was so amazing. Still to this day I long for it. I don't know if you have ever had a perfect one-on-one relationship with God, but I am here to tell you that it is 100 percent possible. In fact, until you reach that, I don't think anything in this book will ever help you beat anything.

I mentioned earlier that I had been married several times before, and in all those relationships, I had always had a sexual relationship prior to marriage and would not even think of anything different. However, my relationship with Katie was the exact opposite. We wrote to each other almost daily while I was a student at Teen Challenge, so in her own way she was going through the same things I was going through. One of the first things that struck me as kind of odd was that we were to pray on our knees every morning from seven thirty to eight o'clock; it was a requirement. I found that strange. I wondered how on earth anyone could do it, and the first time I attempted it was to no avail. I lasted only about seven minutes. I sat there wondering how this could be important (remember, pray without ceasing). Over the next several days, I found myself making a list of things I needed to pray about. I even wrote down four basic steps to prayer:

1. Address God.
2. Thank him for the blessings (things) you have.
3. Ask him for what you need.
4. Then close in the name of Jesus Christ.

Before I knew it, I was praying for fifteen or twenty minutes, and pretty soon I caught myself running out of time. Thirty minutes was not enough time to cover all the issues I needed help with in my life.

I remember telling Katie how amazing this daily experience was and how I actually did feel different every morning. I challenge you to try praying for thirty minutes each day and see what happens in your life. If we pray, he will answer us, no matter how big or how small the issues we pray about are.

We at Teen Challenge were having the time of our lives, and then heart attacks number one, two, and three occurred within a twenty-four hour period. I found myself on a gurney in the emergency room being taken away for a procedure to install a heart catheter. I was all alone in a different state with no family or friends. It was scary, to say the least. Then the doctors informed me that my outcome should be okay. They had placed two stents to correct two blockages in my heart. I was relieved, but then they said that I had much more severe heart problems. I needed a new heart valve and an aneurysm repair on my aorta. (You may recall that earlier I had prayed for God to make me physically sick at the sight of drugs.) I knew that the Teen Challenge ranch could not allow me to return simply because of the liability it would incur.

It was terribly disappointing to know I had to leave Teen Challenge. It's a Christian-based rehab program, and upon completing it, participants can become ordained ministers and teach at any of the program's two hundred-plus facilities. Beyond that, I can't begin to explain the feeling of having a safety net for the first time in my entire life. I was in my early forties, and it was the first time I had ever felt safe. I was walking with the Lord every step and every day of the week. But leaving was a decision that had to be made. I realized that my prayers to become sick at the sight of drugs had finally been, without a doubt, answered. It is very difficult to explain how I felt and still feel knowing I had actually prayed these heart attacks and all that I was going through on myself. But how else could I sit here and say that I truly know that it was an answer from God that I could not and would not deny? And still, to this day, even after almost losing my life, I feel it was the biggest blessing ever bestowed upon me.

I called my Katie and asked her to come to California to pick me up so I could begin to face what was ahead of me. I was in need of one of the most dangerous surgeries known to man. Being diagnosed with an aneurysm is pretty scary. An aneurysm occurs when a section of the artery or vein—in my case, the ascending aortic artery-balloons out because that certain part has weakened. It enlarges and can explode at any time, at which point a person would literally bleed to death internally in less than two minutes.

To top that off, my aortic valve was leaking to the point that it made me feel as if I were having a heart attack all the time.

So with all that ahead of me, I felt the need to ask God if that was the time to marry my best friend, Katie. Crazy, I know, but it seems that every time I am in the middle of a life test, I have a huge blessing waiting for me. It's kind of like in the Bible when the Lord promises us that if we do his will, we shall be "blessed beyond all measure." I want to make sure that you not only take from this book the lessons I have learned but also that God has your back no matter what situation you're in. I promise you that this statement is true. This point in my life relates to step number five: expect the miracle.

After Katie and I were married, we found ourselves homeless. I had no job, and my health was not good. I went to the VA hospital since I was a veteran and had public health care at my disposal. I was admitted to the hospital for the next two weeks and placed in the surgical intensive care unit (SICU). I don't think I can properly explain the fear I was feeling. We were homeless and jobless, and our prospects looked like hell. I began to test the five-step program that you are reading about. I was an addict and was doing everything I knew to do. I was practicing what I am preaching. As a result, I was able to see firsthand how this five-step program worked. I followed the steps and prayed without ceasing.

When I was released from the hospital after the heart attacks, the doctors said they wanted to see if the aneurysm was growing or not before they elected to do the surgery because the procedure was as life threatening as the condition. Katie had a car, so we traded it in for a car of lesser value and were able to rent an apartment for one month and still have transportation.

If you remember, I had earlier worked for a company in Seattle and Hawaii and made more than a hundred grand a year. I called my contacts there looking for work only to be told that they were not interested because I had been arrested by the feds. They didn't believe I was clean, let alone sober.

As a side note, there is a difference between the two. To be clean is merely to do without the drugs. To be sober means you are choosing a sober lifestyle. Once you're healed, you're healed, no questions asked. Ever since I began practicing these five steps, I have not had even one dream about my past. In fact, it's almost like a foggy light off in the distance, almost like it never happened. When you're caught up in that vicious cycle, you not only feel hopeless; you also feel so alone.

When you hear of people who have undergone cancer treatment and gone into remission, they don't ever refer to it again as having cancer. Rather, they say, "I am a cancer survivor and have been healed." I really think that it's a must to stop referring to yourself as an addict in recovery; rather, refer to yourself as having been healed from your addiction. It is so important that you feel as if you're a new creation. Throughout the Bible, God refers to healing in some form or another sixty-nine times. That's a lot. If he healed people then, why wouldn't he heal us? Are we any different from any one of them? I say no. In fact, I say we are chosen to live in the times we do. We must change our entire way of thinking. We must understand that God has a part in everything in our lives.

Programs alone won't work. Unless something of great importance takes place and a healing occurs, you are doomed to death with this addiction. The healing I am speaking of can take place. Without it, you're not going to stay clean (in remission). I have treated and continue to treat my life as a rare blessing. Because I have allowed God into my life, something amazing has taken place and I am free from all addictive behaviors and drug use. It has happened only because God has let it happen and because I allowed him into my life completely. Some readers might not get the message of this book simply because they don't believe there is any hope for their situations. If you're one of them, that's where God wants you to be because he wants complete submission to his will. Only when you allow him in and let go will you feel his presence. I can't find the words to define or express the feeling that you get once you are actually there. It means so much to me to just breathe every day. I guess until you have reached the point in your life when nothing but being healed from addictions matters, you will continue to gamble with your life. It is my true belief that, in this life, one can become normal and that's not all that bad. We all have been given special gifts, but some of our lifestyles have covered up our gifts to the point that we can't even recognize them anymore.

When I was living in my addiction, I would always find a way to get high no matter what. Even when I had no job and no money, I found ways to keep up my habit without fail. If you can put one tenth of the energy that you put into getting high into life instead, you will make it. In my case, I have a hard time understanding God's will, so an exercise I do almost every single day is to try to look at my relationship with God as if it were a relationship with my earthly father. I never really had much of a relationship with my earthly father, and that makes it that much nicer to have one with my heavenly father. If you can somehow put it into terms that simple, you will find it a little easier to maintain that relationship and listen to your heavenly father.

Once you have established a belief, and I mean a real belief, in God, you become dependent on his inspiration. It begins a relationship like none other. He's there for you no matter what. He wants you to succeed.

I know it's hard to take that first step down the right road of life, but I am here to tell you that once you have, God won't abandon you or ever forsake you in times of need. I can remember time after time trying every single thing at my disposal to stop using drugs. I would have a little success with not using, but at the first sign of any adversity, I would get higher than ever before. And with each relapse, it would take longer and be much harder than the time before to get clean again. What I want you to take from this chapter is a belief that God is there to not only support you but also to help lead you in the right direction. You can't fail when you have given your will up to be his will.

# Chapter 9

## Don't Spin Your Wheels

Working in the automotive field for the past fifteen or so years, I have learned a thing or two. I have learned that an engine and a transmission have to work in perfect harmony in order for the power to be distributed to the transfer case or rear end and make the car move. It's the same way with God's will: in order for the power to be distributed equally and for you to move to the next phase in life—a life with meaning and happiness—you have to work in perfect harmony with God's will.

If anyone in the world knows how hard it is to wait for God's timing, it's me. In fact, I wrote the book on impatience. But I would encourage you to take it slow. Don't rush into anything new and hard. Allow this new life you're leading to bring you the joy that God designed it to bring you. It is hard to believe that one plug can make a motor run like crap. In line with that example, it's hard to believe that missing one morning of reading God's word or even praying can make the rest of the day run like crap.

So how do you avoid spinning your wheels? It's easy—ease up on the gas. Life is not a race to the finish line, nor is it a look-what-I-can-do event. So when you're stuck, stop mashing the gas pedal. When I sit down and consider how involved higher powers are in my life, it makes me want to dance and shout.

How do you ease up on the gas? Well, if you're in a rut and feel like you're getting nowhere, step back and look where you have been. It will shock you to see how far you have come in such a short time. It is also important that you read and pray daily until you get unstuck. I am not saying you should read the Bible in a day. Go to a local Christian bookstore and get a daily Bible-reading plan. One thing my wife and I do daily is pray both in the morning and at night. Believe it or not, I still pray without ceasing in addition. Another thing we do is listen to nothing but Christian mainstream music. It's amazing; I haven't listened to any other kind of music in two years, and I don't miss it at all. Also surround yourself with great people. My dear, sweet mother-in-law sends me a morning e-mail every day, and in it is a special message from Jesus that she shares with me. It makes my day so much more enjoyable. Once again, I surround myself with eagles. You know the saying, right? "It's hard to fly like an eagle when you're sleeping with the chickens." I have made many attempts to stay away from any stories of my drug days. I have not talked about my connections with any cartels, the amounts of drugs I used, being arrested for running dope, or being charged with running a prostitution ring. Instead, I have tried to show you and tell you that there's nothing shy of murder that I haven't done or seen done. So if I can do it, so can you.

In the Bible, the Apostle Paul was a "murderer of Christians." With that said, I promise you that there is a place for you here in God's fold. The reason for staying away from the sources of the information on my rap sheet, or what my wife calls my resume, is that it's evil and in my past. I don't like it spoken because I respect the devil that much; I don't want him anywhere near me. The reason I chose to include it here is so that you can see some kind of light at the end of this long tunnel you're in.

# Chapter 10

## Sick and Tired of Being
## Sick and Tired

This is one of my favorite sayings. I picked it up during my recovery, but it never meant anything to me until I laid in SICU for a week, hanging on for dear life. Now it means a lot to me. Let me tell you what I get from it and maybe you'll get it as well. When I hear it, I look back to all those times that I was so out of control and lost. I can remember waking up in places with other people whom I didn't even know. One time, I was left at a person's home for four days while my friend, who was my ride, was out looking for dope. All I did was shoot up. Every single time I stopped using, I would get fever and an upset stomach. I finally got sick and tired of it. Now, when I look down at my "zipper" — that's an eight — to ten-inch scar about a quarter of an inch wide — it makes me sick.

On May 20, 2010, I arrived at the veterans hospital around six thirty in the morning. (Have you ever wondered why they tell you to be there so early when all you do is sit there and wait?) This was definitely a day that I will never forget for as long as I live. I had such a bad feeling that things were not going to be okay. Every time I would attempt to tell my wife that, though, she wouldn't hear of it. She kept telling me over and over, "God's in total control." I remember trying so hard to somehow hold on to that belief, but I couldn't.

If you knew you were going to be in an accident that could take your life in an hour, what would you say or do? Well, my "car wreck" was less than an hour away, and I was terrified, to say the least. The nurses proceeded to prep me by shaving my entire body. I remember that when my dad had open-heart surgery, one of the things that upset me so much was that the intern who shaved him was cutting off his moles and didn't even seem to care. I mention this because of all the memories I have, good and bad. Anyway, as I lay there getting ready for this surgery, I had so many fears and so many unanswered questions racing through my mind. I asked my wife to lean over so I could tell her something. In a soft whisper, I said, "Could we please go home? I don't think I am going to make it through this procedure. Please, please, stop them. I don't want to do this."

She said with much confidence, "You will be fine, I promise. This all will be well." It's not that I didn't trust God; it was that I was facing death as a result of choices I had made during my addiction. The part that really scared me the most was that my heart would not beat on its own for a projected four hours. (In reality, it turned out to be over nine and a half hours.)

I remember being wheeled away, but that's it. As it turns out, I didn't do as well as they thought I would. I lost a tremendous amount of blood, had to have six blood transfusions, and was on life support for almost a week. Isn't it funny that even when we are faced with things we feel could turn out badly, somehow we find comfort in them? When we went into this, we were told that the life support would be taken off almost immediately after the surgery. Not in my case.

So here comes the good part: did I have a vision? Is this where God came to me? Did I see the light? Well, the answer to all of the above is no, but something really amazing did happen to me, something that would change my life and ultimately be the impetus for this book. My wife told me that I went in and out of consciousness after the surgery and would try to pull out the breathing tube. I remember during the first night in the hospital seeing this nurse standing in the corner of the room. I found it really strange because she never helped out; she only stood there. I fell into a deep sleep because of all the pain meds and somehow found myself standing up and looking at myself in the bed. The first thought that came to my mind was, *Wow, great dope.* I decided to walk over to the nurse in the corner, and wouldn't you know it, she was my mom. I hugged her, and her smell was the same smell she had her entire life. It was a perfume from Avon. It is so strange to me that I can remember her smell. I found comfort in it when she would hug me as a child.

I wanted to know everything, and all she said was, "Hold on. It's not over yet." When she was on her death bed, I had asked her to come back to me from time to time, so I was excited. As I said earlier, I was and am a mama's boy. I was the baby of my family, and I truly took advantage of that when Mom was around. My addiction got so bad that I lost contact with my siblings right when my mother passed away. I had an older brother whom I adore and had really missed for more than four years, but I knew that we would forgive and forget someday and wind up living out our last days on this earth together. I mean, he was like a father to me, so I knew we couldn't continue to stay apart. But my sister, my only sister, I had lost some seven years before due to my addiction. I knew that one was going to be tough. You see, I had always lived with her during my summers, and out of everyone in my life, I felt that I had let her down the most. I can't explain it except to say that she was my world and her approval meant everything to me.

So at a time like that, I really needed to have that motherly touch. I hadn't spoken to my sister for years, but when I came to, the only thing I could do was write the words "sis here." My wife contacted her—how I don't know—but she explained to her that I might not make it off life support and could die. I stood there with my mom for days. I can't explain it. I could see my body lying in that bed, and I could see all the nurses tending to me. I could even hear the alarms going off. I remember seeing my wife, who, come to find out, hadn't left my side in over four days, balled up in the chair next to my bed.

I told my mother about her and what was going on, how I had wanted to become a minster, an evangelist. It seems like I did all the talking, but I can remember her telling me I had to go and lie down. I explained that I didn't want to, and she said, "You have to. God's not finished with you yet."

I woke up and looked at the door, and in walked my beautiful wife and my sister. She had left her job as the VP of a bank pretty much without permission and flown twenty five hundred miles to see me. As I write this, tears still roll down my face. It's something words can't explain. I remember telling my wife that her love would save me if it got bad. Thank God she was able to interpret my message.

When they came back the next morning, I was sitting up and eating ice cubes. If you'll remember, I have taken the approach of viewing addiction as a disease, and as such it is curable or healable by faith, just as the blind man in the Bible regained his sight. Therefore, I proclaim in the holy name of Jesus that you are healed. I promise you that amends are not necessary; God has paid for your sins, and you are not an addict. Rather, you're in remission from this addiction. If you speak and believe it, it is recorded in heaven.

Since then, I have moved nearer to my sister, and we have restored our relationship so much that we are partners in our own AAMCO franchise. I could write another book on her alone. All I will say here is thank you, my sister, for loving me even when I wasn't lovable.

Being raised the way I was, I had a firm belief in life before the one on this earth, a life with God, and being Christian, I believe in a life after the one on this earth, also a life with God. I hold these beliefs on complete faith, but having had a near-death experience, I now see things differently than before. It's almost like the veil between lives became a little lighter.

Throughout this book, I have stated that I prayed my heart problems on myself. I want you to know that I believe that. I needed to go through all of that to be able to tell you about the experience. I remember so well how I always felt so useless and never had hope for life when I was an addict. It's important that you recognize this as the devil. If you think about it for just a moment or two, if what I am saying is true—that a war is being fought for souls as we speak—it is absurd to not think that the devil will do anything and use anybody, even family, to win his battle for your soul. In this world, turmoil sprouts up daily, and despite all that, nothing is more important to the devil than your soul and your failure in this life. If you take the approach in this book, it will not only shed light on a much bigger picture, it will also help keep you clean from this disease.

# Chapter 11

## Katie's Chapter

My husband asked me back in November 2010 if I wouldn't mind adding my side of the story and what I personally went through with his open heart surgery in May 2010. Since then, I've been debating and contemplating whether I should put my thoughts and feelings into this book.

When I was growing up, my mom always told each one of us girls that God has someone special set aside just for us. After my father passed away back in 1996, I guess you can say I rebelled a little. I just didn't care. I had lost my father. Little did I know that it was just my earthly father, not my heavenly father, my eternal father. God was with me the whole time.

I met my husband one March morning in 2009 when my family picked him up for church. That day, my mom began to tell me things about his past. The more she would tell me, the more I wanted to know. I spent a little bit of time with him until he left for Teen Challenge in June 2009. At that point, we began to write to each other and talk to each other almost every chance we got. He would tell me things about his past, his running and gunning. But that was just it—it was his past. The more we wrote and spoke to each other, the more and more in love I became with him and he with me. I knew that, without a shadow of a doubt, this was the man that God had set aside just for me. I began to pray, "Father, if this is the man for me, please make things happen smoothly." My prayers were actually answered. You see, once he went to Teen Challenge, I became closer with God. I began praying daily, began reading his word, and began giving things over to him and expecting the miracle to happen. I continued the prayer: "Father, please, if this is the man that you have set aside for me, please make it happen in your timing, not ours." You see, Jay and I thought that he would continue at Teen Challenge, graduate, and then go to the Teen Challenge Ministry Institute to study and become a minister. But God had other plans for both of us.

July 2010 is when our lives began to change. Jay had one heart attack after another. I was in another state and became worried and stressed. I just didn't know what to do. He had a procedure called a heart catheterization in which doctors go in through the leg and send a catheter through the femoral artery and up to the heart to examine and determine what needs to be done. Little did any of us know that this was only the beginning of the battle. God doesn't put things into your path that you cannot handle.

I went to get him without the consent of my mother, who actually forbade me to go down to Teen Challenge and pick him up. She kept telling me that he needed to do this alone. I would tell her, "No, he is family. This is what family does; they are there for each other." So I went down and got him. The next nine to ten months were filled with doctor appointments after doctor appointments. They told us that the aneurysm wasn't big enough to operate on but that he also had two leaky valves. They finally came to the conclusion that they were going to go in and fix the aortic valve, which should take care of the mitral valve leak, and while they were in there, they would fix the aneurysm too.

Finally, after months of debating, they set his open-heart surgery for February, which got switched to April and then finally to May. I knew from the get-go, and he told me, that if I did not put my complete and utter faith and trust in God, he would not pull through the surgery. I believed him, and I believe that is why God chose to postpone his surgery—because I just wasn't ready.

I have believed in God from the time I was very little. I remember being baptized, but I never really put my complete trust and faith in him. And that is what he wanted and so patiently waited for.

May 19, 2010, was the night before Jay's open-heart surgery. I guess you can say that I was ready but wasn't ready. I had to keep reassuring him that everything was going to be okay because God is in control. We needed to put our complete, 100 percent faith and trust in him. Of course, the devil had him thinking that he wasn't going to make it. I told him, "I have given this over to God, and I have not and will not take it back. God is going to guide the surgeon's hands, and everything is going to be okay. You will wake up from the surgery and recover with flying colors." Yes, I put my complete faith and trust in him; no, I was not taking it back; and yes, I was expecting the miracle to happen. But a little part of me was not only reassuring him—I was also reassuring myself. I can remember lying on the couch with him while he was weeping and telling me, "Please don't make me do this. Please. I feel like something is going to go bad. Something bad is going to happen. I can just feel it."

After only about three or four hours of sleep, we woke in the morning, grabbed our packed bags, and drove ten minutes to the VA hospital. During the drive, I was praying to God silently while Jay was on the phone with his brother and his sister. We got up to the hospital, and we were both emotional wrecks. I hid my emotions because I had to calm him. As they began to prep him, the doctor came in along with the anesthesiologist and surgical nurses, and they started to prepare us for what was about to happen. Both of us started crying. The doctor/surgeon told us that Jay would be out of surgery by four o'clock at the latest, would be put into SICU, and would be off life support by morning.

The entire time we were listening to all of this, I was praying, "Father, please guide the surgeon's hands, and thank you for placing this obstacle in front of us." Did I actually thank God for allowing my husband to go through open-heart surgery? Yes, I did. I believe that we face the things we do each and every day because he has placed them in our paths. I remember sitting in the waiting room with a customer from work, anxious, stressed, and worried. I tried to occupy my time by calling Jay's family in Florida, and I prayed continuously.

Every time the nurse came out and told me something, I got on the phone with his sister or brother or aunts or cousins. Three o'clock rolled around and was soon long gone. Once four thirty hit, I began to become frantic. I thought, *Oh, my god, what is going on? He should be out by now.* I went to the window and asked for an update, and the nurse told me to go back to the waiting room and that she would send somebody out to talk to me. It seems like I was sitting there for hours, but in reality it was only about ten minutes. Someone came out and told me that they had to open him back up; he was bleeding from his chest tubes more than the doctor would have liked. At about six thirty, the surgeon came out and pulled me aside. He said that the surgery had gone smoothly; he had replaced Jay's aortic valve and fixed his aneurysm. When he began to warm Jay's body up, his heart started pumping on its own. That was our biggest fear, that they would have to shock his heart. As the doctor walked away, I breathed a sigh of relief. I already knew that it was going to be a long and hard recovery, but I didn't realize what was ahead of us.

I grabbed everything and went over to the SICU waiting room, waiting to see the man that I was actually going to spend the rest of my life with. Fifteen minutes went by before he was rolled by on a hospital bed, his arms strapped down, a huge bandage on his chest, a urine catheter in, a machine that regulates the blood coming out of his heart cavity, chest tubes, and a machine that was actually breathing for him. I never could have prepared myself for what I saw. My heart was in despair—it was weeping—but I was thanking God that he did not take Jay from me. There my husband lay, basically lifeless but so full of God. I can remember being allowed to go back and stay with him in SICU. When I walked into his room and looked at him, he was so pale yet so full of life. As I sat beside him and held his hand, I began to talk to him and tell him, "Honey, everything is going to be okay." He could hear me, but he couldn't.

That night was treacherous. He would come to enough that he would cough and try to pull out his breathing tube. As the next day rolled around, I began to get frantic because the doctor told me that Jay's blood oxygen levels were severely low. Every time we tried to allow him to breathe on his own, the more we had to increase his dependence on the breathing machine afterward because of his oxygen levels. He tried to talk to me, but he couldn't because he had the breathing tube shoved down his throat. The next day, I thought that maybe, just maybe, he would be taken off the breathing machine, but, boy, was I wrong. God chose to keep him with him for just a little bit longer. The doctor told me that, because of what he had done in his past, his lungs were not expanding to their fullest capacity. All I can remember is sitting there day in and day out, relying completely on God because I couldn't help my husband. I would try talking to him but would get so frustrated because the nurses would tell me not to, saying he needed to relax and keep calm. You see, the more anxious and excited he would get, the more pain he would be in and the more medicine they would have to give him.

I was standing next to him sometime on Sunday, and he wrote on my hand, "sis here." I asked him, "You want your sister to come see you?" He replied by nodding his head. I immediately called his sister and told her that she needed to come. I said, "Your brother isn't doing well, and he wants you by his side." She was able to book the next day's flight from Santa Rosa Beach, Florida, to Salt Lake City, Utah. The doctors kept telling me, "Hopefully tomorrow he will be able to get the breathing tube out." But then they had to put in a feeding tube so he could get the nutrients he needed.

Monday rolled around and, yet again, the breathing tube stayed in. At that point, I was getting so frustrated, but I knew that if I didn't put my complete faith in God that Jay's health was going to deteriorate instead of improve. I thanked God each and every day for giving me another day with my husband, who had lived such a hard and rough life. By Monday, all I wanted to do was take him home and take care of him myself because I believed that I could take care of him and watch over him better than any doctor or nurse could, but that was not true. His sister, whom I had never met before in my life, arrived at the hospital at about six o'clock at night. I met her halfway down the hall, and we embraced almost like we had known each other for years. I thought, *Finally, I'm not alone*, although I had not been alone at all; I had God there with me the whole time. As we walked the thirty steps to the room, I prepared her for what she was about to see, but no words could prepare anyone for that. As we walked in, he woke up and saw her, and all three of us began to weep. I could see the joy in his eyes at finally being face to face with his sister, whom he had not seen in years. I could see life in him, which I had not seen in days.

Before the surgery, Jay had made me promise him that I would not leave him at all while he was in the hospital, so I became frantic and began to weep hysterically because the doctors were literally making me leave on Monday night. I tried explaining to them that I had made this special promise and that if he woke up and I was not there, he would panic. They took my number and promised me that if he did panic and they couldn't calm him, they would call me back in. They said that he was going to have a long, hard recovery and that I needed my rest and strength. I had gone from Thursday, May 20, to Monday, May 24 without eating a single thing and drinking only water. So on top of being tired, I was hungry and so very weak.

I walked into his room in the SICU the next morning at seven o'clock, and he was sitting up in bed. They were giving him minimum amounts of medicine, they had his breathing machine turned down to the point that he was doing the majority of the breathing on his own, and he was actually awake and alert. They told me that he did so well during the night and that his oxygen levels had improved so much that they were taking him off life support at ten o'clock. I called his sister to share the news, and neither one of us could believe it. Sure enough, ten rolled around, I stepped out of the room, and they pulled him off the machine. I walked back in, and he was breathing on his own—no breathing machine and no feeding tube. I thanked God for answering my prayers. From that moment on, he kept improving and improving. It was a miracle that only my heavenly father could give me. Within days, he was transferred to the regular floor, and finally, after fourteen days in the hospital, I was able to take him home and take care of him with the help of God.

Little did I know what was in store for us. As we drove home, each and every bump put him in excruciating pain. What normally took ten to fifteen minutes to drive took a half hour. Over the next three weeks, neither one of us slept nearly enough. He would run such high fevers that I could not for the life of me break, and I would have to literally drag him out of bed and take him up to the hospital for physical therapy. He was not able to use his arms at all to prop himself up, so I had to brace his back and neck and lift him up into a sitting position. He had to lie on his back for months, and he couldn't even wipe himself for weeks after his surgery.

Earlier, I had made a very special promise to him—that if he made it through his open-heart surgery, I would take him to Florida, where his family was. His sister, brother, aunts, uncles, and cousins all lived there. Sure enough, once we got the go-ahead from the doctor in August 2010, we packed up our Magnum and drove across the country with everything that we owned in the back to Panama City, Florida.

He will pay for his past for the rest of his life. Since the Florida trip, he has been in and out of the hospital numerous times with chest pains, emergency heart catheterizations, and most recently a staph infection, for which he had to go in twice a day for ten days to get IV antibiotic treatments because of his heart valve.

As I look back over that year, I know that it was difficult but so worth it. God has given me the chance and the blessing to live another second, another minute, another hour, another day with the man I hope and pray to spend the rest of my life with. Through the last couple of years, I have continued to believe in God and have put my faith and trust so strongly in him that I have expected and received the miracle of being able to wake up and live another day with my husband.

Having never been addicted to any drugs or alcohol, I have never been able to relate to what addiction is like, so imagine my surprise at realizing that everything you just read about was a fulfillment of the five steps in this book. I want to make you this promise: I have seen, felt, and lived through more during the past two years than ever before in my entire life. These five steps are truly of God and only God. I promise that if you work through them, you can get through anything, whether you're an addict or not.

# Chapter 12

## Is Enough, Enough

I remember all the cool sayings I would pick up in the twelve-step meetings and how I would call my sponsor with them. One of my favorites was "I am sick and tired of being sick and tired." I am asking you: are you sick and tired? I want you to know that my sponsor is Jesus the Christ, the son of a living god, and he is available to listen twenty-four/seven. I promise you that with these steps, you won't need anyone's help but God's. I know what you're going through—in fact, I dare say that I have been through much worse—but that's not important. What's important is how you begin the process. I want to help you one more time, to show you how it's done. Pray with me:

> God, I am so sorry for all I have done. Sometimes I believe you're there, and then at other times I don't. I need help now. I have been told that if I will talk to you every day, every chance I get, and turn over what I am battling, you will heal me. I promise you, God, that I won't under any circumstances take it back from you. I will expect the miracle of healing. I have been using a long time now, God. I turn it all over to you. Make me unable to buy drugs. Make all the people around me leave, and surround me with the people I need to become a better person. And God, since drugs are a sin and addiction is a disease, I want you to know that I believe in the blood of

Jesus and I hereby accept his blood to pay for my sins and my transgressions.

If this prayer doesn't make sense to you, then let me explain what I am trying to say. It is most likely the case that what you're doing now is not working, correct? Well, this will. I promise you that what I am trying to show you is how simple God wants you to be when asking for help from him. Talk to him like he is your father; after all, he is. Throughout all history, God has always spoken to his children. Why would he stop now? There is one requirement one must meet to be successful with *I Surrender All,* and that one thing is pray now. Open your heart and watch what happens. The power that you're praying to tells the ocean just how far it can come onto the shore and tells the moon where to hide when the sun comes out. Those words are so amazingly sung by Nicole Mullen in the song "My Redeemer Lives." I think this is the point where you need to venture out on your own to start the most amazing journey you have ever dared in your entire life.

Don't let the devil win. You can do this. I did it, so I know that you can as well. I can honestly say that I am healed from my drug addiction and that I have never been more successful, more happy, or more full than I am today. It's truly a life God wanted me to have.

So many times, we take for granted what we have been blessed with. In many cases, families are torn apart by the choices we make regarding the drugs we take into our systems. The most important thing I have learned from all these experiences is that I have to somehow gain a belief that there will be something after this life is over. If you can actually believe that there is nothing after this life, that it's over when you die, then this book and program will not work at all. By my faith, I know something awaits us after this life. It only makes sense, if you think about it. Why would we be put on this earth and live a long life only to have it all be over? That can't be true. We have to have the hereafter.

Now, in other programs, they say that somehow you have to gain a knowledge of your higher power and that it can be anything. I say no; it has to be God and his son Jesus Christ for by him and through him is the only way to stop drugs and never relapse. I know what you're going through. Trust me; I know what that feeling is like when the boredom sets in and you actually have to start making choices on your own. Are you ready for that? As I have said and will continue to say, you can have a relationship with God unlike ever before. God intends for you to be successful at everything you try in life—in love, in money, in everything. If you stop and think about it, that is a very bold statement, but it is completely true. God loves you so much, and help is finally here.

# Chapter 13

## The Vicious Cycle

The vicious cycle that addiction brings is one that takes all prisoners. I know you have heard it said that someone or something takes *no* prisoners, but that doesn't apply to addiction. I have often just sat and wondered, *My god, why don't my kids want to be a part of my life? I have so much to offer them. Why would they not at least try?* Only recently did I find out why. I never knew how messed up someone could become on drugs of any form. This applies especially to the hard stuff—meth, coke, and heroin. I call them the big three.

I am here to tell you that alcohol, pot, overeating, and abusive relationships all fall under the same heading as the big three do. Because I had never been on the other side of this cycle that I am on now, living a life that is worthy of blessing from God, I never knew its true power and its effects on everyone, but especially kids, siblings, and parents. I have once seen the effects on a parent dealing with one of his kids' struggles, but I had never understood what it is like for children.

I have mentioned that I wanted to try to be in one of my kids' lives. I have never seen children being ripped from the homes they know, nor have I seen how kids want to be ripped from their homes until recently. The story I am about to tell is one so close to my heart and so personal that I am almost hesitant to put it in this book.

I have an older brother who is the complete light of my wife's and my life. We enjoy him so much. He is getting up there in age and is the kind of man who you want to just sit next to because you love him that much. I reflect on my life and realize everything

I have ever learned from my brother, Zane, like driving, playing tennis and basketball, and shooting. For almost every single thing I ever learned, he in some way was the person who taught me.

One of the most enjoyable things in my childhood was watching wrestling on channel four every Saturday at five thirty. To this day, I can still remember every single wrestler's name. I had a great mom, but my dad wasn't anything close to a real dad. The closest thing I had was my big brother, Zane. Even the name is amazing, isn't it? I mean, who wouldn't want to be named Zane?

He knew of this love I had for wrestling and loved me so much that he would drive thirty miles round trip out of his way to pick me up so we could drive another forty miles to see live wrestling. In fact, we even had ringside seats. As you can imagine, I missed this man greatly while I was lost in my addiction. He has always made every attempt to love me no matter what, but after I got fully into my addiction, he decided he had had enough. For more than seven years, I didn't hear a word from him at all.

Now, we see each other almost every single day. I can credit the fact that I didn't get beaten to death by my dad to my brother's saving my life. It seems that we have always lived together, worked together, and just been with each other, off and on. One of Zane's children is, shall we say, running amuck and has been running from the law for a couple of years. He has three amazing children—a set of fraternal twins and a six-year-old boy. Well, to make it quick, my wife and I have the chance to be blessed with Zane's son's twin girl.

## Not Knowing What to Do Next

One of the most confusing things about trying to live a life of some value is not knowing what to do once you are clean. The actual day-to-day stuff that will keep you sober has to be addressed and, in my experience, learned, just like learning to walk. This is because for so many years, you have practiced and lived in antisocial behavior. As a baby, you didn't just get up and start running everywhere you went. Rather, you first learned how to trust the person or persons trying to teach you how to walk. Notice that I didn't say you first learn how to stand; I said you learn how to trust. Your mom or dad held you, loved you, and then tried to stand you up. That, believe it or not, is learning how to trust someone.

It is that same trust that you must have to get over this addiction and begin a relationship with God. Learning this trust will lead you, just as when you were a baby, to stand on your own and to learn how to walk. It is so important that we always remember that we were not born knowing how to run; we had to learn it day by day. There is a familiar term—"blind faith." Do you think for a minute that when this country was formed, the Founding Fathers knew what it would become? I say the answer is no. What is so amazing about unknown or blind faith is that along with the fear of not knowing comes the fear of unknown blessings that lie ahead of you. Everything that we do in life has a reason tied to it. We are that type of people; we always want to have something in return. I wish we could be different, but we're not. From the time we start school, we are taught that with good grades come rewards instead of being taught that with good grades comes great knowledge. So it is not easy to live life not knowing what's around the corner. What has helped me is that I have made every attempt to work on one thing at a time. I have focused on my relationship with God, and a lot of the other stuff has worked itself out. I mean, for so many years living in addiction, we don't care what happens to us. But then, all of a sudden, we get a job and maybe start a relationship. Then what do we do? I say don't worry about the not knowing. Work on you and you alone, and then move on to the next thing that needs work.

One thing that helped me when I first became sober was to never go to places where I used to get high. I changed my friends. I even recorded a voice mail greeting on my phone that said, "Hi, this is Jay. I am out making changes in my life, so if I don't call you back, please consider yourself as one of those changes."

I guess everybody is different. A lot of people won't even worry about the not knowing, but I always want to know what lies ahead. So if you have that same problem, just remember that you're not alone.

# Chapter 14

## Avoiding What God Wants

As I have said throughout this book, God is awaiting your request to become a part of his fold. What is it that you think God wants for you? Is it a life of misery? Is it a life of nothing but pain and sorrow? Is it a life that is always spinning out of control? For most of my adult life, I have avoided what God wanted for me. I never felt I was a part of anything of value whatsoever. As I look back, I can't recall one single time that I ever felt equal to anyone, let alone as gifted or talented as them. I searched for years before I was healed, trying to find out what went wrong with me in my life that made me an addict. I really wanted to know why God would allow me to be this way. I was not normal. And do you know what? I never found out why I was the way I was. All I could find out was that I wasn't allowing God to be God.

What does that mean? The god I am talking about is a god of immeasurable love. So why didn't I feel it? How could I not feel his presence? It was because I wasn't allowing him in to be who he is. If you believe in God and go to him in prayer, say, "God, I need a new job," and then sit there and wait, I promise that you're going to remain unemployed. But if you go to him and say, "Father, I need a job. I have done this, and I am doing this. Please bless me with the inspiration to look harder and closer so I may get this job I want." That is allowing God to be God and not avoiding his direction or his desires.

One of the biggest pitfalls of addiction is the not-feeling-adequate syndrome. It will get you high again faster than anything else; I promise you this. I said earlier that I was the type that would mess up a good thing just because I felt that I was not worthy. I would meet a girl and then run her off, thinking that it wasn't going to work anyway. It's very important that you recognize this as a tool of the devil, plain and simple. It's a tool that is and can be used by the devil and cause you great sorrow. It will even cause your demise if you're not careful.

So with that said, it's time for you to learn how to gain a sense of self-worth. It's not as hard as you might think. I do simple things to help me feel better about myself. Every single day, I try to find one good thing I can do for someone else that will make me feel God's presence and, in turn, allow me to feel good about myself. I tell myself things I like about me, which allows the spirit of God into my life. I also catch myself looking in the mirror and telling myself that I am a new creation each and every day. But out of all of the things I can and will do, nothing in this world works better for me than to read his word so I can feel his love as the words flow from my mouth, letting me know that God loves me so much that this is what he's done for me.

Recently, I was confused about what to do with regard to a huge decision I was facing. I kept trying to weigh the options and then take it to God in prayer. I worried and worried about what I thought God wanted from me so much that I went to my mother-in-law and said, "Mom, what do I do with this?" Without hesitation, she replied, "Sounds like you need a little more God and a lot less Jay."

I was praying so much for help with this decision that I was not allowing God to be God. Instead of praying for more of God in what was going on, I was praying for God to answer me now, please. I catch myself overlooking what I have been given; in fact, I almost look at my blessings as a burden, not a gift—like I'm unworthy of so many blessings. I will try to explain. When you have all these new feelings you will have as the drugs leave your system and you feel them right down to the tips of your fingers, they will tend to scare you and make you feel like you don't know what to do with them. It is very important that you try in every way to see God in what you're doing. This is without a doubt the most important thing people have to do: find God in what they are seeking, in what they are saying, and in what they are doing.

In this new life you're living, so many times—even more than ever before—you will be tempted to the point of no return. It's then that you must seek God in everything, including the temptation you're going through. By seeking him, you will find him. Doesn't that make sense? How many times have you been so focused on your next fix that nothing could get in your way? That's the kind of focus you must have when seeking God and seeing God in everything you do. I am not trying to sound like a broken record, but statistics show that you're going to fail at this addiction-recovery thing at first, so I am repeating this God thing because it has healed me from what I thought was an unhealable addiction to meth and cocaine. I was told I would never stop using, but I have. And that's why I am telling you to let God be God in your life. Allow him to work the same miracle in your life that he has worked for me, and you too can stop using and become a new creation in the eyes of God.

# Chapter 15

## Living Life to the Fullest

One of the most common mistakes that people make is that they forget that this life was and is intended to bring us joy. It is so important that we, whether addicts or new creations, believe in this statement. We are entitled to joy just as much as any other one of God's children, no matter their past or present. God loves the sinner as much as the saint. I think that sometimes, because of the choices I have made, I feel so unworthy of the joy life is supposed to bring me. I think, *I can't possibly be this blessed* or *Life can't possibly be this great*. Well, it is, and yes, I am, as are you.

As I mentioned in the last chapter, don't allow your blessings to feel like a burden. Don't feel that if you become successful, you're not worthy of the success. I am a firm believer in that old saying, "Don't say it or it will happen." If you allow doubt into your mind and out of your mouth, then your entire life will become filled with doubt. I have told you that God is real and that your life depends upon a personal relationship with him. I can't begin to express how true that statement is. Your life truly is dependent upon your relationship with your father in heaven.

So how do we get that relationship started? It's simple: pray and then include God in all we do from the time we wake up until we go to bed. Include God in the process of your day. I find myself thinking about God and what he is like throughout my day. I find myself praying when no one is around or, for that matter, in my head when people are around. So many people make God unreachable. Please don't do that. If you only could see where your life will be six weeks from now if you start this true relationship with your father, you wouldn't need this book. In fact, you could be writing it yourself. God is so reachable that it will come to feel like he's only a phone call away. With that said, I encourage you to consciously keep him in your thoughts until you find yourself doing it unconsciously.

I look back on how many times I have been on the other end of what I am saying now and think, *Am I getting this right, Father? If not, what do I say?* I am not a person who goes into anything lightly. In fact, my friends have always said that I am known for the "go big or go home" attitude. So how did God finally get it through my thick head? Well, he damn near killed me with the heart attacks. To this day, I am still paying for the choices I once made during my addiction. My health is still not good; I have had two mini strokes and am on a drug called Coumadin, which attacks the part of the liver that makes the blood clot. So if the level of that medicine is too low, my blood will become too thick to pass through my metal heart valve and put me at more of a risk for a major stroke. And if the level is too high, then I could bleed to death internally. God had to humble me almost to the point of death. So is that what is keeping me clean? No, it's not. I merely have finally gotten that relationship with my dad (God) that I needed to have so that I would feel enough love from him to choose this new life he's given me. It is true that you have to allow God into your life. It's also important to remember that you're a new creation in God's eyes.

There are stories in the Bible that will blow your mind. In one, a woman was on her menstrual cycle for years and believed in Jesus enough that she knew that if she could only touch him, that bleeding would stop. When she attempted to approach Jesus, the crowds were too large and she was forbidden from going near him. Through her faith, she made her way close enough to Jesus that she was able to touch only the very edge of his robe. And when she did, Jesus felt the energy drain from his body and said, "Who has touched me?" This woman—this mere, common woman—spoke up and said, "It was I, Lord," and then Jesus looked at her and said, "Go and want no more, woman. You have been made whole" (Mark 5:25-34 NLT).

In this day and age, it is a little harder. We have to have more faith, but we don't have to have Jesus in the flesh. He is still with us and will heal you. I swear it is so.

# Chapter 16

## Surround the Camp with People Who Know God

If I may give you a piece of advice on how to live life after you have stopped running and gunning, it is to surround yourself with people who want the same things you want. It is so important to not only be around these people but to make every attempt to follow their lead in everything you do on a day-to-day basis. In a traditional twelve-step recovery program, they suggest getting a sponsor. In this program, Christ is your sponsor, and I would encourage you to also identify a person or people who have what you think is a wonderful relationship with God. The Bible says that "by their fruits you shall know them" (Matt. 7:16 NLT). It's hard to be an angel if you live with the devil, and it's hard to be sober if you're living in a crack house.

I have made some bold and powerful promises to you, but I am warning you that change must come for this to continue to work. If you have worked through this program and have truly become a new creation, then you know that you could not remain one if you are surrounded by the same people who can't help but be a negative influence in your new life. I will be so bold as to say that you have to do away with these people until they get to where you are now. I have a friend, as I mentioned earlier, whom I do not call or associate with to this day not because I am worried about using; it's that I know he's not where I am in life. I will avoid even the appearance of anything evil because I respect the presence of the devil. I have come too far to allow Satan in my life in any way. I miss this friend and love him with all my heart, but all I can do is love him and pray without ceasing for his recovery.

I have another friend, Loren, with whom I have actually spent time behind bars, and we talk almost every single day. Why the difference? He is where I am in life. He's a new creation. I am so blessed to have not only strong friendships but also a wife who is my entire world. She was raised correctly. She is not at all experienced with anything related to the drug world. She has never been high, never been in jail, and never had anything remotely close to an addiction. It's really amazing. However, she can still relate to me and everything that I go through. I could write an entire book on her and what she has done for me.

I am also blessed with her mother, from whom I have gained so much strength that I would dare say God made her just for that purpose. Having her now as my mother-in-law is amazing. I hope you see what I am trying to tell you. People will be placed right where you need them by God himself if you allow God to lead the way and let God be God. I also want you to remember that a man can be judged by what he does when no one is looking. As you start your day, try to remember this one thing: with every step you're taking, you're not alone. As I have said already, help is here. I encourage you to surrender all to God.

And follow these five steps:

1. Identify your god.
2. Pray without ceasing.
3. Give it all to God.
4. Don't take it back.
5. Expect the miracle.

# Conclusion

I hope that you have taken from what you have read some kind of hope that there is a life that is worth something and that it's waiting on you to live it. I can never forget what kind of hell I was in when I was actively using drugs. I thought it was fun at first, but I couldn't foresee the total disaster that lay ahead. Let me give you an example. I was raised in the South along the coast, where storms are common and some bring tornadoes. Have you ever seen a tornado? It will leave you in awe. All the power and excitement that are generated from the cyclone are amazing, but as soon as it passes you by, nothing but pure devastation, raw disaster, and yes, sometimes even death lie in its path. Addiction is that way too. At first you don't intend to harm anyone or, for that matter, even yourself. You're just getting high. But then it grabs you, and it won't let you go. That is when the bad stuff begins, when the kids are forgotten, families are forsaken, and relationships are destroyed.

I pray that you see what is as plain as the nose on your face: you are not now and never will be able to live a worthwhile life doing what you're doing and using what you're using. When I set out to write this book, I pleaded with God for hours for the strength to do this task. I asked God to inspire me and to actually bless my mind and my ability to tell the story of what I have been through. I hope you can see that help is right here in front of you. I am counting on you to trust me when I say that God is real. I bear personal witness that his son, Jesus Christ, is real and did die for us to pay for our sins. God is our father and is so happy to know that you're trying to change. I promise you that if you will work through the five steps, you will be blessed.

So with that, may God's richest blessings be upon you until our next meeting. To get a peek at that, please go to http://www.heavenlyoaksretreat.com. And always remember the steps:

1. Identify your god.
2. Pray without ceasing.
3. Give it all to God.
4. Don't take it back—any of it. No matter how well it's going, don't take it back. It's going well because of God, not you.
5. Expect the miracle.

He will work in your life daily as you start down that road of recovery. I want to close this book with this claim: "Nothing at all in this world is placed before you that God has not already given you a way to do."